Shooting's
Strangest
Days

Shooting's Strangest Days

TOM QUINN

Extraordinary but true stories from two hundred years of shooting

ROBSON BOOKS

This edition first published in Great Britain in 2002 by Robson Books,
64 Brewery Road, London N7 9NT

A member of **Chrysalis** Books plc

Copyright © 2002 Tom Quinn

The right of Tom Quinn to be identified as the author of this work has
been asserted by him in accordance with the Copyright, Designs and
Patents Act 1988.

British Library Cataloguing in Publication Data
A catalogue record for this title is available from the British Library.

ISBN 1 86105 500 5

Typeset by FiSH Books, London WC1
Printed by Creative Print & Design (Wales), Ebbw Vale

Contents

A DEATH FORETOLD

NORFOLK, 1800

One of the most curious tales in the whole history of shooting concerns Lord Andover who died in 1800. Lord and Lady Andover were members of a party staying at Holkham Hall on the north coast of Norfolk. It was arranged that a day's shooting would take place on 8 January of that year, towards the end of the time that the guests were gathered together.

That morning a white-faced and clearly shaken Lady Andover stayed in the drawing room while the men gathered ready for the shoot. Her husband then appeared and announced that he would not be shooting that day. When he was pressed for an explanation for this last-minute change of plan – which surprised everyone as Andover was a very keen shot – he explained that his wife had dreamed the night before that he had gone out and on the third drive his gun barrels had burst and he'd been killed.

Everyone present tried their best to make light of the dream, but no amount of persuasion would convince Lord Andover that all would be well if he went out with the other guns. 'I'm not in the least worried myself,' he said, 'but my wife is very upset and I will not risk upsetting her any further.'

By lunch time Lady Andover had recovered from the fright the dream had caused her and she told her husband that she no longer felt nervous about his safety. His lordship then announced that he would join his companions for the afternoon's shoot and he set off with a servant and his two favourite dogs.

Half an hour later he arrived at Creake Farm about five miles from Holkham Hall. He had an idea the other guns would be in the area and he had every hope of catching up with them, but as it turns out he never saw them. At about 1.30 p.m., having failed to put up any game, the two dogs suddenly pointed and Lord Andover moved towards them cocking his double-hammer gun. Then one of the dogs ran in and put the birds up too soon. Lord Andover decided to tell the dog off so he handed his gun to one of his servants. Just as he stooped to catch the dog, the gun the servant was holding released a hammer and fired into Lord Andover's back. He fell to the ground and bled profusely but remained conscious. He was carried to Creake Farm and a messenger was sent to Lady Andover who arrived soon after. When he saw his wife Lord Andover simply said: 'Dear, your dream has come true.'

As soon as the doctors saw Lord Andover they knew there was nothing they could do to save him as the shot had penetrated one of his lungs. He died two days later in his wife's arms.

KING OF THE PICKLES

SHROPSHIRE, 1810

John Mytton was variously described by his contemporaries as the maddest squire in England or as Mango, the king of the pickles, whatever that meant. He was High Sheriff of the county of Shropshire as well as M.P. for Shrewsbury for a number of years. The fact that he almost never appeared in the House of Commons can be attributed entirely to the fact that he was addicted to shooting, hunting, practical jokes and extremely dangerous escapades.

His favourite sport was probably hunting but he was an enthusiastic shot with a particular passion for shooting wildfowl.

Mytton lived at Halston near Oswestry. Here in winter he would get out of bed in the middle of the night, take off his flimsy nightshirt and set off completely naked but carrying his favourite gun across the frozen fields towards his lake. Here he would ambush the ducks, fire a few shots and then return to bed apparently none the worse for his ordeal. He frequently got up again half an hour later – presumably after he'd warmed up – stripped off and went through the whole process again.

When he went on more formal shoots in winter and on the coldest, frostiest days he wore a few light bits of clothing to save the other guns' blushes, but cursed at the pointless formality of wearing clothes and insisted that it reduced one's chances of shooting anything. As a compromise he would turn up at a shoot wearing a thin linen nightshirt and a pair of fine leather slippers. He could never be bothered with underwear or a coat of any kind. His most extraordinary day's shooting came when, out shooting alone and while stalking some ducks that had settled on his frozen lake, he got fed up waiting for the birds to come within range, stripped naked, sat on the ice and then slowly shuffled forward on the slippery surface until he was within range. It took over an hour but he never caught a cold or seemed in the least unwell after this or indeed after any of his naked shooting exploits.

When he wasn't shooting Mytton drove his carriage round the local villages hurling money out of the windows. If he was planning a journey to London he always filled his coach to a depth of two feet with hazelnuts in order that he and his companions (if he had any) should not go hungry on the way. He disliked jumping fences on horseback and tried regularly to get his carriage and horse over a fence – and was nearly killed on several occasions. He drank several bottles of port every day of his life and despite being continually drunk for years on end was a fine marksman.

Mytton bit horses he didn't like, tried to ride his pet bear round the estate, hunted his horses till they dropped dead and shot everything that moved on his estate. By the time he died aged just 38 he'd shot all his game and given away or spent every last penny of a fortune that in today's values amounted to some £20 million.

PRACTICAL JOKER

ENGLAND, 1815

Shooting men are not all devoted killers whose every moment is spent wondering how they can improve their marksmanship in order to achieve ever greater bags. Many are happy family men for whom shooting is a social event, a chance to catch up with friends, and shooting men enjoy nothing as much as a good lunch, good conversation and – unfortunately – practical jokes.

Early in the nineteenth century Lord Alvanley and Lord de Ros were out shooting together. They normally had a bet or two on who would shoot what or how big their bag would be. Normally they also gossiped about their friends, planned their country house parties and, having known each other since childhood, were the best of friends. But Alvanley was a noted practical joker and eccentric and when de Ros suggested that, for this day's shooting, they should agree to carry what the other shot, he must have been delighted. Half an hour into their day's shooting he spotted a donkey and promptly shot it. How Lord de Ros got out of his side of the bargain is not recorded.

STAND AND DELIVER

HOUNSLOW, 1820

Even today the name Manton brings to mind some of the best guns ever made. Joe Manton was making guns long before Purdey was ever thought of, but Joseph Manton made all kinds of guns: shotguns of all bore sizes from 4 (big enough to bring down the biggest elephant) to 28 (as light as a walking stick), but he also made pistols and rifles. Most of his pistols were for personal protection at a time when there was only a rudimentary and often corrupt police force. Travellers were always particularly vulnerable – indeed it was said that on a journey from London to Norwich a man had at least a fifty-fifty chance of being attacked and robbed.

But back to our gunmaker, Joe Manton.

He'd been travelling across Hounslow Heath in Middlesex along the main road from London to Bath. The Heath had for centuries been famous for its highwaymen and thieves, but for those travelling west there was no avoiding it. Manton was travelling on business and as it was daylight he thought he had little to fear. Then the coach lurched to a halt and he heard the dreaded shout 'Stand and deliver'. Manton stuck his head out of the carriage window. He found himself staring down the barrel of one of his own guns. Arguing with a highwayman, even for an instant, was usually fatal, but Manton was so outraged he could not keep silent.

'Why damn it, you rascal!' he reportedly bellowed, 'I'm Joe

Manton and that's one of my pistols you've got. How dare you try to rob me!'

'Oh,' replied the highwayman coolly, 'you're Joe Manton are you? Well you charged me ten guineas for these pistols, which was a damned swindle, though I admit they're damned good barkers. Now I mean to be quits with you. Hand over ten guineas and I'll let you go because you're Joe Manton, though I know you have at least fifty pounds about you.'

Speechless with rage, Manton swallowed his pride and handed over the money, but he never forgave the highwayman for effectively getting a pair of his pistols for nothing.

To make sure it never happened again he made himself a special double gun with barrels nearly two feet long. Whenever he travelled he carried it with him and he always called it the highwayman's master.

Many years later a highwayman again stopped him. This time he was travelling towards London, and as good as his word, he whipped out his special gun and shot the man dead. History does not record if it was the same highwayman who'd taken his ten guineas all those years before.

STIFF UPPER LIP

SUFFOLK, 1848

Maintaining a stiff upper lip was something of an obsession among our Victorian and Edwardian forebears. It all stemmed from the idea that an Englishman – certainly if he believed he was that now forgotten thing, a gentleman – couldn't bear to appear to make a fuss, even if he'd just had his leg shot off in the trenches or was about to be hanged.

One famous incident occurred in which a young lieutenant berated a corporal (they were both about to be shot by the Germans) for blubbing: 'Don't make such a fuss man,' he is reported to have said. 'You would have died eventually anyway.'

That was the sort of attitude men also admired in the shooting field, which may explain why, when Lord Francis Hope accidentally shot himself in the foot at a pheasant drive, he insisted on finishing the drive. He must have been in great pain, however, as the foot later had to be amputated.

In an extraordinary coincidence, Hope's brother, the Duke of Newcastle, shot himself in the foot a few years earlier in similar circumstances. Once again, when his loader and cartridge boy rushed to his aid he told them both not to embarrass him by making such a damned fuss. He could learn to hop as well as the next man and that's just what he did – once they'd amputated his foot.

At a very grand shoot in the same year, 1848, a beater lost an eye in a bramble bush. When one of the guns expressed his sympathies for the man, another gun – the earl of something or other – said: 'Oh, he's a hard man. He doesn't care about his eye.' In the same year the Duke of Gloucester, a very wild shot, deprived his equerry of one eye, and then complained that the man made 'such a fuss about it'.

1848 was an unlucky year for shooting because in that same year an old gentleman in the eastern counties shot and killed a boy and an underkeeper. He was asked if he wasn't terribly upset by the two deaths 'Well,' he answered, 'I wasn't too bothered about the boy – I gave his mother five pounds – but I was dreadfully upset about the man. So much so that I didn't go shooting for a whole week.'

LICKED TO DEATH

SOUTH AFRICA, 1850

In the 1850s reports reached various European settlements in Southern Africa that an African out shooting with an old flintlock shotgun had met with a most extraordinary death.

Since he had been shooting alone the exact details of what happened had to be pieced together later on, but the basic facts at least were clear.

He had gone out hunting alone with an old, very rusty rifle owned in common by the men of his village. The villagers had had little to eat for weeks and as their best hunter he had set out to try to provide some food. Why exactly he went alone no one knows.

Judging by the distance between his home village and the place where he was found he must have tracked a group of animals for some considerable time. From the evidence of hoof prints in the area it was also deduced that he had been pursuing buffalo, but the buffalo – or least one of them – had clearly pursued him. From the state of the body and the accounts of local hunters the sequence of events was probably as follows.

The hunter had spotted a group of buffalo – probably quite a small group or he would not have risked tackling them alone – and had spent the day tracking them over almost a dozen miles. He may well have eventually decided to try to shoot when, coming within range, he spotted a straggler. He must have wounded the animal very slightly as no traces of buffalo blood were found. But the animal charged the hunter. Unable to reload and fire again quickly enough the hunter had run for it and reached a big projecting rock, under which he hid, just as the buffalo caught up with him.

What followed was just another example of the kind of behaviour that made the buffalo more feared in Africa than either the rhino or the elephant. First it tried to gore the hunter by pushing its head under the rock, but the gap was too narrow for its massive curved horns. Then the buffalo must have spotted the hunter's leg. This would have been easy as the gap under the rock was so narrow that the hunter had only been able to get under it at all by lying lengthways. But a patch of the hunter's thigh was very close indeed to the edge of the rock and though the buffalo couldn't reach it with his horns he could reach it with his tongue. And that's what he did. He began licking the bare patch of flesh and he licked it with his massive sandpaper-textured tongue until it began to bleed. He licked on after the blood started to run and continued until most of the muscle lay bare and the blood flowed profusely. The hunter could do nothing. As the buffalo would not go away he could not come out from under his rock and he couldn't escape the buffalo's tongue as there was no room under the rock.

No one knows how long it must have taken the buffalo to lick down through the skin and then the fat of the leg and into the muscle, but it must have been hours. One can only hope that the hunter lost consciousness soon after the blood began to flow and death would probably have come quickly after that. He was tracked and found three days later.

CANNON AGAINST POACHERS

WILTSHIRE, 1852

Shooting, like hunting and fishing, has always produced – or attracted – eccentrics and none more so than Colonel George Hangar, who ran his own enormous shoot, but never invited anyone to shoot it with him. After several poachers were chased off his property and his breeding pens were disturbed he decided to take matters into his own hands.

He decided that the best form of defence against poachers was attack. First he had a six-pound cannon specially made, which he bolted on to a platform high above the roof of his house. The house was at the edge of his wood with good sightlines along the rides.

Having built his cannon, Hangar bought several huge sacks of marbles – the sort children play with. He then moulded hundreds of clay balls, each about the size of the bore of his cannon. He took these to be baked at the local brick kiln, first boring three or four holes in each. The holes were about the diameter of a finger and they were bored right through each clay ball.

Hangar loaded his cannon with two handfuls of marbles followed by a couple of clay balls. On the first occasion he spotted what he thought was a poacher he fired the massive load. The noise was indescribably terrifying – a sort of deafening whizzing, followed by a noise like the rattle of a machine gun as the marbles cut through the leaves and branches of the trees.

Hangar also built his gamekeeper a house on the opposite flank of the wood. The poor old gamekeeper's house had no door or window of any kind on the ground floor. The lower rooms were lit from windows fixed at special angles on the first floor and the front door was situated ten feet from the ground. The idea was that the keeper could draw the ladder up at night safe from any possibility of a revenge attack by poachers.

By his keeper's house Hangar built a thirty-foot-tall round tower with another six-pound cannon mounted at the top of it. A walkway connected the keeper's bedroom to the top of the tower.

The idea was that virtually all the wood was within range of the two guns and, just to make sure that the local poachers knew they meant business, Hangar and his keeper fired continually into the wood day and night – which effectively ruined the shooting anyway.

INDESTRUCTIBLE BEAR

INDIA, 1852

Bears in the northern mountainous areas of India had a reputation for fearlessness in the face of man and for having developed, curiously enough, a taste for mutton. English sportsmen who wandered these areas while on leave from the army at the end of the nineteenth century often wrote about bears killing two or three sheep or goats at a time and then simply disappearing without eating them. On other occasions a whole sheep would be eaten at one sitting. For this reason – and perhaps because they still seemed so common – there was little sympathy for the bears and the prevailing view seems to have been 'the only good bear is a dead one'.

In *Shooting in the Himalayas* published in 1854 an anonymous author, who must certainly have been a British soldier, describes how pheasants were pursued in the Himalayas for their beauty and because they were good to eat, tigers were pursued because they were somehow seen as the ultimate quarry and the poor old bear was pursued simply because he was a nuisance. It is therefore rare to find an author paying tribute to this much-despised animal.

But if it was despised no one doubted its ferocity and toughness, as witnessed in one extraordinary incident by our anonymous soldier author. He'd been shooting for several weeks without much success, although he lost a few beaters along the way to disease and accident, when he came across a steep and narrow ravine. Two miles into the ravine, he noticed

14

on a ledge high up and some distance ahead a large black bear that appeared to be rummaging around in a few scant bushes. The soldier took aim, fired and the poor old bear tumbled off his ledge, but the soldier knew he hadn't actually hit the bear. The bullet had bounced off the rocks above the bear's head causing it to jerk upright and lose its footing. Without touching the sides of the precipice the bear fell over 200 feet. The soldier wasn't in the least worried, thinking that, although he hadn't killed it with his bullet, the bear would be killed by the fall. How wrong he was. No sooner had the bear hit the ground than it sprang to its feet and charged. The soldier and his beaters ran for it and were lucky to escape with their lives.

CAUGHT ON THE MOUNTAIN

NEPAL, 1855

Shooting, it may surprise many, is not a dangerous sport at all – fewer people are killed while out shooting than out fishing and the incidence of accidental death among horse riders is staggeringly bad by comparison. But shooting can be dangerous in ways that have little to do with the business of firing a gun. Shooting in remote places is dangerous simply because large animals are dangerous: also, one may fall or be cut off by bad weather. Even the most experienced are sometimes caught napping, as it were.

The Puthan tribesmen of the Himalayas are among the toughest people in the world and when they go out to shoot tahr and ibex they know exactly what they are doing, but in an extraordinary incident in the 1850s a Puthan tribesman lost his life within earshot of the safety of his village.

He had shot a tahr but it had run some distance after being hit and he had spent a little too long finding it. When he did track it down he found that it was high on a rocky ledge above his own village. He pushed the dead animal over the ledge and it was collected by his friends from the village below, but as it was now dusk he was unable to find his way back down the way he had come, nor could he even escape the narrow ledge on which he found himself. He called down to his friends in the village below and explained his situation.

They lit fires hundreds of feet below and shouted continually through the night to keep him awake, but their efforts were in vain. Cold makes a man sleepy and, despite knowing that if he fell asleep that sleep would be his last, the Puthan stuck high on the ledge could not resist the pull of unconsciousness. In the middle of the night he finally dozed off and, as there was no room to lie down on the narrow ledge, he slipped over the edge and fell to his death below.

RIDING LION

SOUTH AFRICA, 1857

In 1857 William Cotton Oswell spent several months in some of the most remote regions of southern Africa. Almost every day brought something extraordinary as he moved across the plains with hundreds of local villagers carrying his vast quantity of boxes and tents. The villagers had to be fed and it sounds as if Oswell, riding at the head of his entourage with his gun across his lap like a tribal warlord, spent most of his time shooting animals not for their trophies or for the excitement of the chase but simply to feed his followers.

It is clear too from Oswell's own account of this and many other expeditions that the villagers followed him and carried his equipment largely in return for food. Back in their villages they lived at or near starvation point. With Oswell at least they were very well fed as he knocked down as many as a dozen big animals a day.

Oswell tended to ride well ahead of the main party to scout for animals before the game became aware of the vast moving campsite a few miles behind. One day he'd gone much further ahead than usual so he decided to stop to smoke his pipe. He was in an area with clear views for miles – or so it seemed – so he relaxed, tied the pony up and enjoyed his pipe. A moment later the air was filled with the sound of hooves – somehow Oswell had managed to get himself surrounded by a stampeding herd of buffalo. It was one of the few occasions when Oswell's uncanny instinct for self-preservation failed him. But the oddest thing is that, not really knowing what to do, he did nothing. He simply stood as quietly as possible and, probably through sheer good luck, the huge animals thundered by just a few feet either side of him and he was left unscathed.

In all his writings about Africa, Oswell made the point that when he knew the country – mostly in the 1840s and 1850s – game was so abundant that it seemed as if no amount of shooting could ever deplete the available stocks. The inherent fragility of wildlife populations and their habitats was not then known. But the sheer quantity of game – including now rare animals like the rhino – meant that humans were always in great danger if they were mad enough to travel alone or at night. But even during the day sudden attacks by large animals were common and even an experienced hunter like Oswell could come badly unstuck.

A little later during the same expedition on which Oswell survived the stampeding buffalo, he had an even closer shave.

He was out riding alone looking for birds to shoot for the pot when, without realising it, he came too close to a lion that had probably been asleep in some thick undergrowth growing at the side of the path Oswell had taken. The scent of a human nearby would be enough to make a lion attack under certain circumstances, and on this occasion Oswell had barely heard the lion roar when it had reached him. In the instant he glanced back over his pony's haunches he saw the lion rush on to the path, and almost in the same moment, it sprang up at him. Desperately trying to control his terrified pony Oswell gave the lion more time than he probably should have. He later said that the pony's instinct to bolt should have been encouraged more. But as he watched horrified, the lion had in a second leapt on to the back of the pony and Oswell was only spared a severe mauling because the lion had dug its front claws so far into the pony's back that it could not use them to attack him. What happened next was a confused mass of roaring, leaping and terrified squealing from the pony, which lunged and then bolted. Oswell later remembered looking round again and being, at some distant mental level, almost amused to see a lion apparently sitting up on the horse's back and enjoying the ride. The ride came to an end seconds later when the horse thundered under a tree and knocked man and lion to the ground. Oswell woke some time later to find lion and horse long gone and he – by a miracle – dazed and bruised from the fall but otherwise unharmed. To his dying day he never knew why the lion, once toppled from the horse's back, had not killed him instantly.

ROCK-FACE DREAMS

NEPAL, 1857

Climbing high into the Himalayas for weeks and months on end and living in the most arduous conditions – without the benefit of modern insulation materials and lightweight tents – Major Neville Taylor went native when he left his barracks in the south of India and headed north to shoot ibex. When he first began hunting ibex, in what was still a very remote region of Nepal, he wore English tweeds – the sort of thing he would have worn on the Yorkshire moors at home. But he soon realised that the felt and goat-hair shoes, boots, hats and coats of the local people were far more effective on the mountain than the clothes he was used to. Late one evening after a hard day pursuing – without success – the elusive ibex, he and his Sherpa companions were forced to sleep on an exposed hill face while a blizzard came in. Major Neville crept into a narrow fissure in the rock and tried to get some sleep. Soon he was dreaming of ibex and their pursuit and so real did the dream become that, as he dashed across a snow-covered corrie in his mind, he rolled over several times on his rocky bed in the real world and woke to find himself just inches from the edge of the rock face and certain death.

He crept back to his tiny cave and fell asleep again. Still the dreams came and this time he was convinced he was a snow leopard stalking an ibex. The dream was particularly intense, he later said, because of the thin oxygen at high altitude, but whatever the reason he dreamed his snow leopard dream, and crept very close to an unsuspecting ibex. He was prepared to spring and bury his fangs in its throat. Suddenly the ibex looked straight at him and instead of being afraid, as it should have been, to his horror it began to advance towards him and was upon him with one bound. He felt sharp hooves in his back, but managed to seize the beast by the neck while it bleated and he awoke – hitting his head hard against the roof of the cave and realising that in the real world he was gripping real wet wool. What on earth was going on? He ran his hands up to where the horns should have been and realised he had got hold of one of the goats the party took with them for meat and milk. It was snowing hard and the poor animal had crept in for shelter. Feeling pity for the freezing animal, Major Taylor curled up with it and the two slept soundlessly till morning.

BEAR BATTLES

INDIA, 1859

Bears were once common in the Himalayas and the local people were delighted when soldiers, on leave from the heat further south in India, took their holidays in the mountains and reduced their numbers, for inevitably there were conflicts between bears and villagers and the bears could inflict serious damage. Such an idea would rightly be anathema today, but the pressure on the environment was much less a century and more ago.

A particularly keen young subaltern who knew the Himalayas well journeyed there each year from the south of India and spent weeks and months wandering through the remotest regions. He loved the life so much that he always dressed in the clothes of the local Puthan tribesmen. He was almost killed on several occasions either by slipping into ravines or over precipices, but seemed to think real danger was what made the whole thing fun. It was all very different from today's shooting expeditions where the whole trip would undoubtedly be called off if a man were badly injured or killed.

Our young subaltern in the 1850s saw numerous beaters washed away in spate rivers or killed or maimed by bears and simply seems to have accepted it as par for the course.

One evening he and half a dozen beaters were tracking a bear through very thick jungle when, after about three miles, all signs were lost and even the local Puthan tribesmen could make out no signs of the animal, which had already attacked and badly injured two children. They stopped and decided to make camp, but the Englishman couldn't resist wandering off and he soon came to an enormous rock that was partly concealed by thick undergrowth. With an elderly shikari or hunter and a young tribesman he began to explore a cave on the far side of the rock when, without the slightest warning, a huge bear charged out and ran straight towards him growling savagely. The bear threw the young tribesman to the ground and dodged past the soldier who waved a stick as fiercely as he could. The bear vanished before the men could do anything else. When they went to see how badly the young man was hurt they discovered that the bear's claw had gone right into his skull, although he was still conscious.

Apparently Himalayan bears had a favourite trick when attacking humans of swiping in such a way that a claw first ripped the skin from the forehead. Then the whole paw would be brought down on the victim's head and in an instant he would be scalped – the young soldier had seen two instances where bears had removed nose, cheeks and lips at a single stroke. A horrible mutilation, but one that only rarely killed the victim who many might argue would be better off dead after such an assault.

Anyway, on this occasion, the party helped the wounded man back to their base camp some six miles away, knowing they had had a narrow escape, but the young soldier, quite unperturbed by the serious injury to his companion, went on the next day in pursuit of whatever adventure he might happen upon.

CARDIGAN'S FOLLY

ENGLAND, 1859

In the 1850s and 1860s James Thomas Brudenell, seventh earl of Cardigan, was one of the most famous men in England. His fame rested on the fact that, in 1854, he'd led the 'Charge of the Light Brigade' at Balaclava in the Crimea, an event celebrated in Tennyson's famous poem. The poet saw the charge as a heroic sacrifice, but it was actually a most terrible blunder in which the Light Brigade charged heavy Russian artillery at the end of a narrow valley and of 637 men 113 were killed and 134 wounded.

Cardigan's bravery probably had a great deal to do with his legendary arrogance, but in a disputatious and hot-tempered life that included at least one duel he still found time to invent the woollen garment that bears his name.

On the shooting field he couldn't bear to be in the wrong believing that, as a gentleman, he always knew best. He always had to have the strongest, fastest-flying, highest birds or there was hell to pay. He was like a child who had tantrums if things didn't go well, but on a bright day one November in 1859 he finally got his comeuppance.

He'd become increasingly irritated as the day wore on at the lack of birds. Drive after drive produced no more than a few dozen pheasants. At last Cardigan could stand it no longer. He beckoned his head keeper.

'I want you to beat through that wood,' he said pointing towards a thick belt of trees nearby, 'and I want you to do it right now.'

'But my Lord,' spluttered the keeper.

'Not a word, sir, obey my order at once or you will be dismissed.'

The poor keeper hung his head, gathered his men and set off for the wood in question. Half an hour later the beaters were working their way through the plantation and the guns were enjoying the best sport of the day.

The keeper returned to the place where the guns had gathered to congratulate each other, Cardigan busily taking the credit for the best shooting of the day.

'Now sir, will you listen to me next time?' asked the Earl, looking round at his fellow guns with a smile that all too clearly said 'This is why the lower orders need to be kept in their places.'

But when the keeper was at last able to get a word in edgeways he said: 'But my lord – it's not your wood at all – but what was I to do when you told me to beat it through?'

His Lordship's reaction is not recorded.

ELEPHANT'S BUMP ON THE HEAD

INDIA, 1859

A short-sighted old colonel was hunting Bengal tigers from the top of what was reputed to be the most intelligent elephant in India. The animal was famous for sensing when it was near a tiger and would wave its trunk in the right direction and stop absolutely still – like a pointer that had discovered a pheasant – whenever this happened.

As they moved along a particularly narrow ride the elephant stopped absolutely dead in its tracks and waved its trunk frantically, indicating the presence of a tiger a little ahead and to the left. Moments later two tigers appeared just feet ahead of the party perched on their elephant and before anyone could move the bigger of the two tigers launched itself at the head of the elephant and clung there for an instant.

The elephant roared and reared its head, but did not bolt or charge ahead. But the animal's bellowing and sudden shaking threw off the tiger, giving the old colonel, whose presence of mind was in marked contrast to his aged appearance, just enough time to shoot. The first bullet finished off the first tiger while the second missed its target.

All the while the mahout – the elephant's handler – had struggled to keep the elephant under control and it was assumed that his efforts – bashing the poor beast on the head with a heavy blunt instrument – had caused a massive swelling that appeared and grew worse over the days and weeks that followed the incident with the tiger.

The elephant was so greatly liked and admired by its owners that the mahout was in danger of being sacked as the by now massive boil showed no signs of healing and the animal was becoming increasingly distressed by the pain.

Finally the owners called in a vet who lanced the boil while the elephant remained as quiet as a lamb. And who would have believed it – when the boil burst, out popped the second of those two .500 bullets that had been fired at the two tigers.

EXIT PURSUED BY BEAR

KASHMIR, INDIA, 1860

Bears figure largely in the literature of nineteenth-century shooting. The great care they took of their young occasionally caused disquiet even among those who otherwise shot them without a second thought. Now and then the bear turned the tables on the hunter and it is difficult not to smile at the idea of the marksman taking a cool shot, but then finding he has to beat a hasty and often undignified retreat.

When flintlocks were still mostly used by British sportsmen in India a certain captain of the guard fired a shot at a large female bear in a very remote part of Kashmir. He'd been stalking her for hours and was within fifty yards when he took his shot with an old but well-preserved flintlock rifle. Unluckily for the captain the cap, which had probably got damp the night before, merely fizzed a little and the gun didn't fire. The bear turned sharply round at the sound of the gun's hammer falling, but could see nothing as the captain was well hidden behind a large stone. The captain fixed a fresh firing cap to his gun, lifted his head carefully above the stone, took aim again and fired. This time the cap went off perfectly but nothing else happened. The bear jumped and looked round again with a very fierce look on its face. The captain had had the sense to duck at the very moment the cap let out its bang and the bear again did not see him. Astonished at this incredibly unlucky series of events the captain took out his powder flask and put the maximum amount of powder into the

29

nipple to ensure that when the next cap fired there could be no doubt that the powder would ignite. The captain also wiped the gun down as best he could to rid it of some of the damp. When he next looked cautiously over the top of the rock the bear was twitching her ears suspiciously in all directions. The captain knew this would be his last chance. Either he bagged the bear with this shot or she would have a pretty good chance of bagging him.

Again he pushed the rifle up over the stone, but as slowly and quietly as possible – so slowly and quietly in fact that the operation took more than ten minutes. The captain drew a bead on the bear's shoulder and slowly squeezed the trigger. This time the cap fired perfectly with a loud crack, but the extra powder in the nipple began to fizz alarmingly. For a few terrifying moments the fizzing continued then with a loud bang the gun fired, but by this time the captain had taken the stock from his shoulder and was staring dumbfounded at the barrel – the bullet soared uselessly into the air at an angle of about forty-five degrees.

The bear turned instantly on hearing the noise and saw the flash of burning powder leave the muzzle of the gun. With a roar she charged at the captain now cowering behind the stone just fifty yards away. Bears are not slow-moving animals and the captain knew that in about six seconds she would reach him and he would be dead.

In less than a second he turned and raced downhill and away from the bear, which thundered across the rough stones towards him roaring continually. A short way down the hill was a small ravine full of snow and it was so steep that in crossing it to get to the bear the captain had had to dig slots for his feet and hands. The captain reached the snow-filled ravine on the way down with a second or two to spare, for a man is no match for a bear in a running competition. He threw himself on to the snow on his back, lifted legs and feet in the air to reduce the amount of friction and sailed away down the slope faster than the fastest bear could ever gallop.

One hundred yards further down, the steep snowy slope

levelled out and the captain came to a halt. He looked back to see the bear standing on the edge of the ravine where he had begun his slide. She looked alternately at him and then back at the spot where she had left her cubs. She seemed half inclined to continue the pursuit but suddenly changed her mind and disappeared back up the slope. It was the narrowest escape he'd ever had for it is certain that if the bear had caught him she'd have taken his head off with one tap of her huge paws.

LICENCE TO KILL

CEYLON, 1860

Elephants being highly valued animals in Asia, they were only rarely ever shot, but licences were issued when a rogue animal was causing trouble and it was a rogue elephant that nearly killed an Englishman newly arrived in what is now called Sri Lanka.

The young man, a Mr Walker, was an estate worker, who by his own confession became obsessed with the idea of shooting an elephant; something that, despite wide experience of game shooting, he had never done. After nearly losing his life in the attempt to shoot one he remarked that it would have been better in the first instance if he'd seen his doctor about the obsession, instead of trying to satisfy it.

Anyway, he saw in the *Times of Ceylon* an advertisement saying that a licence was to be sold to allow someone to shoot a proclaimed rogue elephant. The animal was said to frequent village lands in the North Western Province within thirty miles of the estate where Walker worked. The temptation was irresistible. So, armed with the licence and a great deal of confidence, Walker set off for the North Western Province. He took with him a rifle that he thought perfect for the job. Arrived at his destination, Walker talked to local villagers who were able to point him in the direction of some paddy fields where the elephant had been seen several times in recent days.

Early the next morning Walker set off for the paddy fields and he must have felt that luck was with him for no sooner had he arrived than the elephant too appeared. It stood in the middle of the paddy field waving a long piece of vegetation. Thinking the whole business of elephant shooting far easier than any book about big game shooting would have it, Walker simply walked to within about one hundred yards of the elephant, aimed at its head and fired. And this is where it all started to go wrong. The .405 Winchester fired straight and true and there seemed to be a reassuring smack just after the gun fired. But the elephant hardly seemed to notice anything. It turned and walked unhurriedly into the jungle at the edge of the paddy field. And that was that. Not realising that the .405 was wholly inadequate for the job, Walker raced into the jungle after the elephant along with his small party of trackers. Despite searching all day they saw no sign of it.

Feeling bewildered and not a little disappointed, Walker returned home but determined to try again for the same elephant the following week.

During the week that followed before Walker was able to return to the paddy fields he began to realise that the problem may well have been his rifle, so he borrowed a .500 Westley Richards and plenty of cordite-loaded cartridges.

When Walker arrived back at the paddy field a week later the rogue elephant was back – but this time he was standing quietly in the jungle at the edge of the field and partly hidden from view. Walker decided that enough of his head was visible for a shot and he duly took his chance. Once again the elephant simply turned and disappeared into the jungle. Walker and his tracker followed the animal for miles and were about to give up the chase when they heard him just ahead. When they came closer to him they realised he was standing in an extremely dense thicket of bushes and bamboo, but by lying down Walker could just make out his legs. Being tired and rather fed up Walker then did something that he regretted for the rest of his life. In a moment of madness – a moment that nearly cost him his life – he fired at one of the elephant's forelegs. Walker thought this would disable the animal and that he would then be able to run in and finish him off. He fired and began to run but within seconds he realised that far from being disabled by the shot the elephant was galvanised into action. Not only that – it was also now really angry and was charging at Walker. Blithely unaware of this, Walker was walking towards the place he thought the wounded elephant would be lying and he had travelled half the twenty yards that originally separated him from the elephant before he realised what was happening. The trackers instantly vanished and Walker simply turned and ran back along the narrow path by which he'd entered the thick bush. The elephant followed, crashing and smashing through the bush and only feet behind Walker, who was as certain as he could be of anything that he was about to be killed.

Just as the elephant was about to crush the life out of him something flashed into Walker's mind – it was something he'd read in a book years before. At the very last minute, with the elephant almost on top of him, he simply turned and doubled back on himself passing just a foot or so to the side of the charging elephant, which passed, he later said 'like an enormous nightmare'.

Too terrified to stop, Walker kept running till he could run no more, but the elephant never turned to pursue him again and simply carried on in the same direction, the noise of its crashing growing ever fainter. Soon the trackers reappeared and Walker returned home a sadder and wiser man, but he hated the idea of defeat and decided that since the animal had to be got rid of he was the man to do it. He arranged to return yet again the following weekend.

The weekend duly arrived and, armed with the Westley Richards and his team of trackers, Walker found himself once again at the paddy field where the whole adventure had begun. They picked up the elephant's track and set off into the jungle. An hour later he found the elephant that, with its injured leg, had not gone far from its position of the previous week. It fell dead to Walker's first shot, but there was no satisfaction in killing this rogue, he said later, as he had made such a mess of it. He had learned a lesson it is true, but at the expense of the elephant's suffering. He made it a golden rule in all his future shooting expeditions after big game to check that wherever he was during the stalk and after firing the gun he always had a clear escape route.

THE VANISHING POACHER

ENGLAND, 1860

There was a famous Victorian rabbit poacher who evaded the
local keepers for many years. They could never understand
how the man was able to vanish so completely each time there
was a report that a poacher had been seen on the land. Then
someone noticed that whenever the mystery poacher was
around and the keepers hurried to the place where he'd been
sighted a village woman always seemed to be around. It was
only much later that everyone realised the woman was in fact
the poacher.

Buck, as she was known, eventually became so famous –
precisely because women poachers were rare – that she
couldn't poach at all. She was a gamekeeper's daughter and
knew the woods inside out. She'd started to poach after
marrying a man addicted to drink who was never in work and
she was said to know more about snaring and trapping than
any man alive. She knew also how to sneak into a pheasant
wood at night and shoot the birds roosting – and she could
shoot them almost silently. One extraordinary night she
bagged over thirty pheasants with her gun and not a sound was
heard. She later revealed her secret. Her old muzzle-loader had
been adapted to break down into short pieces that could be
hidden in her skirts and she loaded it with tiny amounts of
black powder. On the night in question she used all her
lifetime's poaching skills to get within a few yards of each bird
before firing each tiny charge. She'd chosen a windy night too

so the little puff of sound would be hidden and her clothes were specially adapted with numerous hooks and bags and secret pockets. In these she stowed her birds and shuffled home looking as innocent as she could, though apparently immensely fat.

WIFE MISTAKEN FOR BEAR

INDIA, 1860

Bears in the Himalayas once did huge damage to crops at night and villagers were too poor to properly fence their fields. Their only protection was to shoot the bears. Either the bears died or the villagers starved, it was as simple as that. Many villages built a kind of sentry box – based apparently on the sentry boxes at Buckingham Palace, but on ten-foot-high legs so that they could watch their fields at night and try to scare off any bears without the risk of being killed or injured themselves.

For good or ill it eventually became a matter of honour among the tribesmen of the Himalayas to shoot at least one bear during their lives and one elderly man grew increasingly troubled as he grew older that he had never achieved this distinction. He became increasingly worried that he would die before his chance came so he got up very early every morning and wandered the fields just before and just after dawn in the hope that he would come across a bear that he could shoot. Eventually enthusiasm got the better of judgement and he spent whole nights in the fields so great had his obsession grown. Each time he took an old matchlock gun, probably inherited from the British, and on one fateful night he was just crossing a field very close to his house when he saw a dark shape crouching. He quickly took aim and fired, not realising that the figure in the field was his own wife who was killed instantly. She had risen early to weed the field, but without telling her husband.

In the mid-nineteenth century the Himalayas was still a truly remote region with its own locally inspired rules and regulations that had little to do with the British government a thousand and more miles away, so there was no inquest in this case and the matter ended there.

Death seems to have been far more accepted as simply an unfortunate occurrence in the India of the Raj, as long as the victim was not British of course. Soon after the elderly tribesman accidentally shot his wife, an officer's servant was killed in similar circumstances. He had climbed into an apricot tree when a passing hunter mistook him for a bear and shot him dead. The poor man's friends made a terrible fuss about his death and went to Gholab Singh, the local chief, who dismissed them with the words: 'Why, the man is dead – what can we do?'

ELEPHANT FEAST

AFRICA, 1861

Roualeyn Cumming, a big game hunter who travelled all over Africa during the early and middle decades of the nineteenth century, once shot a massive bull elephant and then watched as local villagers – many of whom had helped track it down – cut it up and ate it. It was a scene that stayed with him for the rest of his life.

First the natives carefully removed huge sheets of skin from the side of the elephant that lay uppermost. Beneath that lay several coats of under skin, which were removed with great delicacy and made into water carriers. The technique used was to cut the skin in big squares and then gather the four corners and edges before attaching the whole thing to a stout stick. These were then carried as far as ten miles distant to water holes, the water being brought to the elephant. The flesh of the elephant was then cut in huge pieces from the ribs before each individual rib was carefully cut out.

The real interest began when the intestines were reached for this is where the elephant stores its fat and fat was most highly valued by the local people. A huge amount of fat was obtained from this particular elephant, but to get at it the men had to climb into the elephant's inside where they literally disappeared from view into the mass of guts.

Hands appeared now and then from inside the bloody mess handing out chunks of fat and while this went on frantic activity round all other parts of the carcase gradually whittled it down to bare bone.

As they worked all the villagers smeared every inch of their bodies from the crown of the head to the sole of the foot with the contents of the elephant's gut as well as blood and other gore. The men were so keen on this that one man would help another by spreading the slimy bloody mess on the other's back. Throughout the entire proceeding there was a deafening babble of voices as the villagers wrestled and elbowed their way frantically inside and out of the carcase. 'It was like a medieval vision of hell,' Cumming later said, 'but it made me realise what ancient impulses hunting stirred, and all the while I stood looking rather absurd with my sophisticated shotgun, open-mouthed with astonishment at the edge of the group.'

THE OXFORD LADIES

ENGLAND, 1861

Westall and Bingley were two remarkable Victorian poachers who caused havoc in the woods of Oxfordshire and Berkshire in the 1860s.

For several seasons in the early part of that decade no one took much notice of the two dishevelled and unkempt old women who always seemed to be smoking their pipes and loitering in the lanes when a pheasant shoot was in progress. Indeed it is doubtful if anyone realised till long afterwards that the two old women were always the same two old women regardless of whether the shoot was at Blenheim or at a remote Berkshire farm. But they seemed harmless enough, dottily jabbering to each other in an incomprehensible language everyone simply assumed was Romany. They often wandered across to the guns offering to sell them clothes pegs or little sprigs of rosemary, or they were obsequiously helpful when it came to lending a hand with the game cart.

It was only when an observant keeper kept an eye on them one day that he realised what was going on. When a drive began one or other of the two old women would wander along behind the guns talking to their loaders or to anyone else who happened to be around. The other old woman waited in the lane and then, when the shooting had begun and no one was taking any notice of anything else, she upped and disappeared. When the keeper followed her he discovered that she was dodging into the edge of the wood through which the beaters were working their way towards the guns. Once concealed in the edge of the wood she lifted her skirts and pulled a very small terrier out of a special bag sewn into her petticoats. Clearly highly trained and like all poacher's dogs taught above all to be absolutely quiet, the terrier immediately began rooting about in the thick undercover. Inevitably pheasants moving ahead of the beaters had already begun to concentrate here and it was easy for the terrier to catch half a dozen of these birds in less than ten minutes. If the terrier missed a bird and it clattered off into the sky, suspicion would not be aroused because it would just look as if the birds were starting to fly because the beaters were getting close to them.

When the terrier had caught a bird he carried it to the old woman who immediately wrung its neck and hung it by a special loop sewn into her underskirts. When she'd secured half a dozen birds the dog would get back into its special pouch and the old woman would wander back into the road and meet up with her friend. They might then hang around until the drive was over before congratulating the guns and setting off for home.

The keeper who'd seen the two women hanging about at several shooting days earlier in the season was amazed at their audacity and the skill with which they caught and hid the birds they'd poached. It was only because he knew what had gone on that the keeper noticed how much bigger one of the two women seemed at the end of the day than at the beginning.

When they were arrested about a mile from the shoot they denied everything and became extremely abusive. 'I'd never in my life heard such foul language,' said the arresting policeman when he later gave evidence in court. 'One of them tried to hit me with one of the pheasants and even a Frenchman might have been horrified at the words they used – pure Billingsgate. We discovered they had a long list of convictions – everything from petty theft to impersonating women of quality.' The two were fined three shillings each.

THE BROTHERS' ESCAPE

INDIA, 1862

Lions and tigers – the ultimate trophy animals during the nineteenth century – were often pursued and shot by professional hired guns after attacking villagers or villagers' animals, but a brave unarmed villager occasionally stood up to a tiger and got away with it.

In northern India a member of the local police – an Englishman – returned to his remote house to find his servant and his servant's brother there. Narwa and Haria had just had a remarkable encounter with a tiger.

They'd been walking along a narrow path through the jungle, Haria leading with Narwa close behind. They'd come to a particularly narrow section of the path, which twisted through tall stands of elephant grass, when Haria heard the unmistakable roar of a tiger and a simultaneous scream from Narwa.

The two brothers were inseparable so Haria didn't think twice before running back. He found Narwa lying on his back with the tiger lying diagonally across him. Narwa's feet were nearest Haria who bent down, grabbed them and tried to pull his brother out from under the tiger. As he did this the tiger stood up, turned to face Haria and growled menacingly, but by some extraordinary chance it didn't attack him. Perhaps it was astonished at this uncharacteristic behaviour. If the tiger had ever seen humans before it would have known that this was not what they normally did. Haria dragged Narwa some twenty

44

feet from the tiger, got his arms around him and managed to get him to his feet after which he half dragged, half lifted him along the path and back to the village. During the first part of the rescue the tiger simply stood its ground and stared in astonishment but growling all the while. Though badly scarred Narwa survived the attack and the local policeman was so impressed by Haria's bravery that he petitioned the king for an award for the man. Sadly other matters intervened and the petition was forgotten. Haria never got his award.

THE LOADER'S REVENGE

HAMPSHIRE, 1862

The loader – the man who took the spent cartridges out of one gun and reloaded it before passing it to the man doing the shooting and then beginning the same operation on the second gun – actually turned shooting into a team sport.

A century or more ago, of course, no one would have admitted this as the loader was a servant and therefore didn't count.

An elderly bishop who was very fond of shooting received invitations from some of the best shoots in Britain and he made a point of taking up as many of these invitations as he could, but wherever he went he always took the same loader with him. He hardly ever spoke to the man and would have intimate conversations with his friends – including members of the opposite sex and his doctor – in the loader's presence. If anyone said anything or complained he merely said: 'But he's a servant.'

Despite this attitude – which today we would deplore – he almost certainly had a high regard for a man who helped him become the best shooting cleric in the country. The loader's speed and timing when he was handling the bishop's pair of Purdeys was perfect – and if anything the weaker link was the bishop who was an above-average shot when on form but rather poor on his occasional off-days.

We don't know if the loader felt patronised by his master's attitude – probably not, since servants generally knew nothing else – but the loader had his revenge on one occasion when he got the chance to put the bishop in his place. They were shooting at a big estate in Hampshire and the bishop was having one of his off days despite the precision loading of his companion.

'Oh dear,' said the bishop, 'we seem to be shooting rather badly today.'

'Yes your Grace,' came the reply, 'and if we go on like this we might just as well pack up and go home!'

RETRIEVING PIGS

YORKSHIRE, 1865

These days spaniels and labradors are the only shooting dogs most people ever use. Spaniels are excellent at rooting out game and pretty good at retrieving it; labradors are the reverse – superb when it comes to retrieving, but less useful when game has to be hunted out. But the modern shooter who tends inevitably to choose between these two breeds is forgetting the history of dogs and sport, for our ancestors were far more inclined to try any dog. Dogs were meant to work and given time, experience and a little luck even a mongrel could now and then turn into a great gundog. So our ancestors turned many breeds into sporting dogs that were hugely popular in their day, although many are now rare. The clumber, for example, is now largely forgotten and whatever happened to the curly-haired retriever? Other breeds that were once used to put up pheasants are still with us but they are known only as delightful pets – few realise that the poodle was bred as a shooting dog and in its day it was one of the most highly regarded. The toy poodle wouldn't be much use in a muddy field, it is true, but the standard poodle is a different matter altogether – he's a sturdy, strong dog with a good thick coat and it is only when you clip him that he begins to look like he ought to spend his life on a silken cushion in a pink bedroom.

Davy Peters grew up with an all-consuming passion for shooting fishing and hunting. He was also a genius with animals who, it was said, could turn any dog into a gundog. He trained terriers and basset hounds to bring his birds back and he once had a bull mastiff that could compete with the best spaniel in the land.

Then one day at a famous estate in Yorkshire he turned up for what was to be one of the most extraordinary day's shooting ever seen.

Instead of arriving on horseback or in a carriage like the other gentleman gunners, he trotted down the lane to the place where the guns were to meet on a well-trained and apparently docile bull. The massive animal, complete with a specially made halter that enabled Peters to steer him, was followed by six full-grown pigs. Each answered instantly to its name when, from his precarious position high on the bull's back, Davy roared out at the top of his voice.

While the various guests stood around drinking gin and water and waiting for the off, Davy's highly trained pigs kept close to him and warned off any intruding labradors or spaniels. When the guests set off for the first drive Davy left his bull tethered in the yard and stalked off across the fields with his six pigs close at heel. One or two other guns became embarrassed at their own occasionally unruly hounds for Davy's pigs were models of good, disciplined behaviour. When the shooting began several of Davy's companions forgot to shoot, so astonished were they by the antics of his pigs. When Davy toppled a bird out of the sky he would choose a pig to collect and obediently the pig named would dash off, pick up the bird and return it to his master's feet. As the day wore on and the guests moved from drive to drive the pigs were used one after another in strict rotation.

For years after Davy always took one or more of his pigs shooting. 'They've more brains in their trotters than most dogs have in their heads,' he used to say when asked about his unusual companions.

Davy's exploits in the shooting field made him famous and eventually he was invited to court. There must have been gasps of astonishment at court when Davy replied to the invitation by saying he couldn't possibly come as he was busy training an otter to fish for him.

THE POACHER'S STOVE

ENGLAND, 1865

John Connell, a poacher active in the 1860s, was a remarkably inventive man even by the standards of a remarkably inventive age. It was almost as if the inventive spirit of the age of railways and engineering had inspired his dim forgotten corner of rural England. He knew that the best time to poach pheasants is when they are roosting, but the wood nearest Connell's home with the richest pickings was also nearest the keeper's cottage. Even a relatively silent .410 shotgun would be too loud. A long stick to whack the birds out the trees would almost certainly make them squawk and alert the keeper or one of his dogs.

What was to be done? Well, with a friend and fellow poacher Connell began to experiment. If I can't shoot them, he thought, I'll suffocate them. He tried many different chemicals and used chickens to test them. The chicken was placed in a cage in a tree and the chemicals were wafted under the bird's nose on the end of a stick or burned in a bag at the bottom of the tree. The tests were inconclusive, sometimes the bird keeled over, other times it seemed more awake than ever. Only brimstone seemed to work consistently well, but brimstone had to be lit and how was burning brimstone to be got to the woods and used there effectively?

Then Connell had a brainwave. He got the local blacksmith to make him a three-foot-high stove that could be collapsed like a telescope. It was cylindrical and tapered at the top. The six tubes from which it was made fitted into each other perfectly. It had a few holes at the top to let the fumes out and vents to allow a draught of air in at the bottom. Fitted with a brimstone candle at the bottom the whole thing could be collapsed and carried inconspicuously under a big top hat or in the folds of an overcoat. The blacksmith also made Connell two lightweight metal poles that fitted into recesses on either side of the body of the stove. These would be used to carry the stove from tree to tree after the metal had become too hot to carry.

The first dark night they tried the poaching stove it worked a treat. After a few minutes under each tree the three poachers who carried it about would hear the soft thud, thud as pheasants simply dropped like conkers. No one knows how long Connell used his stove, but he was one of the most successful poachers of the age who made enough money from his misdeeds to fund a comfortable retirement.

POINTING PIGS

HAMPSHIRE, 1865

Until the late nineteenth-century driven game shooting, organised as it is today, was in its infancy. Most of those who went shooting went walked-up shooting, which is to say they simply walked around till they saw something to shoot. They were usually aided by a good dog, but it was the advent of driven shooting that made the labrador the pre-eminent gundog. The labrador is a great retriever, but he is less good when it comes to walking up game, as he will not 'stand on point'. For the walked-up shooter a dog that would stand on point was, if anything, more important than a dog that would retrieve because it meant that as he walked round he could watch his dog for signs that game had been found.

As soon as it stopped and stood on point it would wait until its master was close enough and then, on a signal, go in and push the bird up and out of the cover. The dog's master would then have a very good chance of bringing the bird down. Good pointers could change hands for a small fortune, particularly if they were also good at retrieving and as the nineteenth century was a time of invention and experiment – right across the arts and the sciences – it should come as no surprise to discover that many shooting people tried to train all sorts of animals to point and retrieve.

In the 1860s a Mr Toomer became well known in the New Forest in Hampshire for teaching a pig to retrieve game, but having successfully done this Mr Toomer decided to go a little further and teach the pig to point game as well. He spent months using a special system of rewards and chastisement at a time when chastisement was pretty much the only tool that animal trainers used. Each time he walked round the woods with his pig – whose name sadly is not recorded – she became better and better at the job until one December day she found and pointed fifteen pheasants and then retrieved them once her master had shot them. It was the first time she hadn't run in too soon. Toomer was delighted, but he soon lost interest and tried to teach a deer to do the same thing. He spent years working with a young fallow and although she never learned to retrieve game she apparently was able to point quite successfully.

STICKING TO YOUR GUNS

DURHAM, 1865

Modern winters really are much milder in general than they ever were in the past if the following story is to be believed. Out one bitterly cold January day on the Durham moors near Sedgefield in 1865 a young man and his friend had been shooting throughout the long day, but it had been one of those days when nothing goes right. They'd had plenty of shots, but hadn't bagged a thing. Every shot was wide and here they were near the end of the day with nothing to show for their efforts. Much of the problem probably lay in the intense cold – neither man could remember a day so icy and it was probably affecting their reactions and judgement of range and distance. Before giving up and heading for home they decided to have one last try for a snipe over a nearby bog. By this time the temperature had dropped even further, but as they reached the end of the marshy ground a bird got up and one of the two put up his gun and tried for it. The shot fell wide. Then, thunderstruck, the young man found he could not remove his hand from the barrel of the gun. The trigger hand that had been on the stock was fine but where the barrels of the gun had rested on the palm of his left hand the gun had stuck fast. The frost was so intense that his wet hand had stuck instantly and immovably to the steel. When they tried to prise gun and hand apart the skin from the man's hand began to peel away and the blood that flowed instantly froze making the situation even worse.

54

Wondering what on earth he could do the young man had an idea. He would put his mouth down near where his hand was stuck and breathe gently to warm gunmetal and hand up sufficiently for the two to be parted. How it happened no one was afterwards able to remember, but in trying to breathe on his hand the young man actually managed to touch the gun barrel just ahead of the glued hand with his tongue. This too instantly stuck immovably. Now the young man was in a desperate plight with his hand and face attached firmly to the front half of his gun and no prospect of releasing either. It must also have been an incredibly awkward and painful position to maintain as the light failed and the temperature dropped even further.

Relief came only after a half-mile walk to the nearest farmhouse, which must have been painful doubled up over a gun. Here a kettle of warm water solved a painful problem, but both hand and tongue had lost a great deal of skin as a result.

DEADLY ERROR

SCOTLAND, 1866

Shooting is inherently dangerous. Yet in an average year statistics show that very few people are killed in shooting accidents. Occasionally, however, an extraordinary combination of circumstances leads to extremely serious consequences.

In a remote part of Scotland in 1866 a group of four friends from the same village were discussing the increase in the number of deer that were damaging crops in a particular place nearby. After the friends broke up two of them decided to get a gun and go to the place they'd been discussing on the off chance that the deer would come that very night. The two arrived at the edge of the group of cornfields where the deer came each night to feed and settled down to wait. They had waited several hours and the coming dusk had made almost everything indistinct when they heard a rustling in the corn just ahead of them. Looking in the direction from which they heard the sound coming they were convinced they saw a large animal moving. The man with the gun took careful aim and waited to get a better sight of the animal. His companion at that very instant saw the flash of a gun from the spot where the deer was supposed to be. In a split second his friend who'd been taking aim fell dead beside him. He himself was also hit badly.

The man who'd fired the shot ran over to them and one can easily imagine how appalled he must have been to find one man dead and another badly wounded. The wounded man lived long enough to testify before witnesses that his death and that of his companion had been caused accidentally and that at the moment when they were shot they were about to fire at the man who'd fired at them.

The man who fired the gun was inconsolable after the accident, his mind and health gave way and within two years he too was dead.

It appears that when the four friends had split up that night each pair had decided independently to try to shoot the deer and it was that extraordinary coincidence that led to the tragedy.

MAD ELEPHANT

MYANMAR, 1869

An old colonel who'd shot for years in what was then Burma described how he hated shooting elephants and that, in fact, they were only very rarely shot and only when they were causing a particular nuisance in one place and couldn't be persuaded to move on in any other way.

This particular old colonel was always called on when a troublesome elephant had to be shot and he had many tales of enraged bulls and near misses. On one occasion he stood his ground as a huge and very angry elephant charged him. His beaters fled screaming but cool as you like the colonel raised his gun and fired once straight at the elephant's head. It dropped stone dead just a few feet in front of him.

On another occasion he had to dodge around a massive tree while a furious bull elephant tried to smash into him with its feet and trunk. The elephant simply succeeded in smashing the tree – which had a diameter of almost 15 feet – into splinters and it was only then that the colonel stepped out and put a bullet into the animal's head.

Despite his long experience the old colonel had never come across an elephant so continually in a foul temper as one animal. For weeks it had been trampling through the villagers' crops and the surrounding woodland. If it saw anyone it bellowed and attacked them, chasing the postman into a shallow cave on one occasion – had the cave not been there or the postman not been very quick on his bicycle he

58

would undoubtedly have been trampled to death.

The village elders had decided that something had to be done, which was when they called on the old colonel and his old Mauser bolt-action rifle.

When the elephant had finally been killed the colonel decided to take a closer look at it. The massive animal measured almost ten feet to the shoulder and had just one tusk but it was huge, weighing almost fifty pounds. The other tusk had clearly been broken off at the root probably in a fight with another tusker. And there in the root of the broken tusk the old colonel found the reason for the elephant's terrible temper – he removed a ball of living, writhing maggots the size of a football. The poor animal must have been in agony. It was no wonder it had become a rogue.

In fact, as the colonel himself always argued, all rogue elephants are found to be suffering from some physical hurt. It may be an infected broken tusk as in this case or, as in another case that involved the colonel, a missing tail. This elephant, which also had to be shot, had a huge mass of maggots in the wound left when somehow or other its tail had been ripped off.

COIN TRICK

ENGLAND, 1870

Trick shooting was enormously popular among Victorians who had heard of the legendary shots of the American West – shots who tended to aim at each other rather than at gamebirds or rabbits. Colonel Peter Hawker, a keen Victorian shot who wrote widely on sport of all kinds, once visited Lord Portsmouth's estate after hearing about the remarkable trick-shooting abilities of a local keeper. He spoke to the keeper, remembered only as Ford, and was most impressed by his ability with a gun. Ford was able repeatedly to put his cocked and loaded gun on the ground, throw two pennies in the air and then pick the gun up quickly enough to hit one penny with each barrel before they fell. Many other guns tried to perform the same trick but Hawker, who knew everyone worth knowing in the shooting world, never saw the trick performed by anyone else. Indeed he spent a long time trying to do it himself and despite his great abilities as a shooter he never once managed it.

FIREWATER

SCOTLAND, 1870

The toughness of keepers – particularly Highland keepers – is legendary and even the more extraordinary stories of their antics are usually found to be true. A keeper from a very remote area was out early one winter morning getting his various bits and pieces ready for the first gentleman stalker of the season. He discovered that he needed some small item that was available in the nearest village three miles away so he set off on foot knowing there was plenty of time as it was still very early in the morning. He would wake the shopkeeper, who was a friend of his, and be back before the gentleman was even out of bed.

At the edge of the village the keeper saw that an old friend was already working in his garden. He stopped to talk to the man and after a few moments accepted the offer of a glass of whisky. He knocked it back, talked for a few more minutes and then carried on towards the village. Ten minutes after he'd left, the keeper's friend realised that by mistake he'd given his friend a glass from the wrong stone jar. Instead of the jar that contained the whisky, he'd pulled out the jar filled with vitriol – sulphuric acid. The cottager was in agonies thinking his friend would probably die. He stood in the road waiting and hoping that the keeper would pass by on his way back to the estate, but no one came and in despair the cottager returned to his house to await the call of the police.

Meanwhile the keeper had arrived in the village, woken the

shopkeeper and bought the odd items he needed. He was then offered a lift back by another shopkeeper who took a different road from the one the keeper had walked – which was why the cottager had not seen the keeper pass by.

A few days later the cottager, still in an agony over the incident, saw his friend the keeper striding along the lane and he ran out to greet him. Before the cottager could say a word the keeper shouted 'Dougal, that was fine whisky ye gave me the other day – do you have more of it?'

The cottager could not believe his ears.

'Did you not feel bad after the whisky I gave you?'

'I canna remember tasting better whisky in my life,' said the keeper, smiling.

'Although there was one odd thing about it,' he continued. 'Every time I sneezed after drinking it I burned a hole in my handkerchief!'

FISH SHOOTING

INDIA, 1870

William Rice, an English traveller in India in 1870, reported seeing an elderly native shooting fish. When he talked to the man he discovered that it was in fact a common practice. Only one species of fish was shot – the murrel, a kind of giant carp.

The traveller asked the village head man if he could accompany a murrel shooter for a day and he was granted permission. The murrel shooter was an elderly man with an old British army matchlock – a shotgun whose action consisted of a trigger that released a lighted taper attached to a small spring-loaded arm. When the trigger was pulled the arm to which the lighted taper was attached flipped forward and touched a small amount of gunpowder which in turn ignited the main charge inside the barrel. When this ignited the shot was discharged and – if you were very lucky – you might hit something. Matchlocks were notoriously difficult to use if you were shooting at a moving target as the delay between pulling the trigger and the gun firing was considerable – at least compared to a modern breech-loader. To allow for this you would have to shoot well ahead of the target. But of course for murrel shooting the time delay didn't matter – as the traveller was about to discover.

The old man led him to the side of a broad river and climbed a gnarled tree that overhung the water. Here he'd made himself a comfortable seat by hacking out a hollow in a fork of two massive branches and smoothing the sides. The old man climbed into the crook of the tree and settled down to wait. He told the traveller that he would be best to watch from the ground but to keep absolutely still. The traveller did as he was told. More than an hour passed and nothing happened. Another half hour elapsed and the traveller began to think this would be a blank day.

Then he noticed ten feet above his head the old man stiffen slightly and, peering into the water ahead of him, the traveller saw what at first appeared to be a black log about two and a half feet long. The log seemed to rise almost imperceptibly towards the surface. As soon as it reached the top of the water the traveller was startled by an enormous bang. The water erupted and a cloud of dense smoke filled the air. The traveller leapt to his feet and rushed to the edge of the water just in time to see the old man bob up through the water with the giant fish in his arms. The old man had seemed too fragile for pretty much anything but he was strong enough in the next instant to hurl the big fish on to the bank, after which he climbed out of the water, picked the fish up, collected his gun and set off for the village with the astonished traveller in pursuit.

The traveller talked to several villagers later that day and they explained that the old man was the best murrel shooter in the village. He was the most patient and would wait for a whole day in his tree if necessary without moving a muscle. His technique apparently was to wait until the very moment that the fish reached the surface to suck down some titbit or other and then fire at it. The trick was not to fire and actually hit the fish. It was apparently far more effective to hit the water near the fish's head and then immediately dive into the water right where the fish had been the moment you fired. When you hit the water you swam immediately to the bottom and there groped about as fast as possible until you felt the stunned fish. This part had to be quick because the fish would remain stunned only for a minute or so. Once recovered it would be gone in a second. For some reason a shot that hit the fish and killed it often resulted in it being much more difficult to find.

The traveller naturally assumed that the percussive effect of the shot hitting the water near the fish was what stunned it but the villagers insisted on another theory: they said that the speed of the shot hitting the water made it boil and the fish then swallowed this hot water and were so astonished by the novelty of it that they forgot to make their escape.

IN SEARCH OF BUSTARD

WILTSHIRE, 1870

Lord Pembroke's shooting parties at Wilton House were part of an extensive and complicated system of social life that involved groups of friends and relatives moving from house party to house party through the season. These were not weekend parties because if you could only get away at the weekend you probably had a job and, in the nineteenth century, part of what defined you as a gentleman was the fact that you didn't work at all. So Pembroke invited his friends to Wilton for Monday to Thursday parties, or perhaps Thursday to Tuesday and as a general rule he knew who was coming and he knew that they knew what was expected of them. Occasionally the system broke down when unreliable types – usually journalists or politicians – had to be invited for some reason.

A particularly thorny problem arose at Wilton in 1870 when Pembroke invited a group of people that included the German ambassador, about whom, of course, nothing was known other than that he was a keen shot. Like many Europeans he had a strangely blasé attitude to gun safety. In fact it was a subject that never crossed his mind. He'd been shooting since the age of five but no one apparently had mentioned to him at any stage that there are certain rules it is a good idea to stick to if you wish to ensure the safety of those around you. Of course no one knew this when he set out on that first morning at Wilton, having told everyone about his skill with the gun and his great experience of sport in general.

At the first drive all went well, although Pembroke was a little concerned to see that the ambassador fired at the very lowest birds and those completely out of range, but at least he appeared to be safe – until the second drive. A flush of good birds seems to have gone completely to his head and he began to swing his gun through the line of guns, firing at random and hitting, over the course of the rest of the day, two of his fellow guests, a dog and several beaters.

Luckily the injuries were not serious, but the ambassador was completely oblivious to anything he might have done – servants and dogs were apparently dispensable – and at dinner that evening he spoke at length about his enthusiasm for shooting and how much he was looking forward to another day in the field.

Pembroke was in a difficult position. The ambassador was an important person and he had no desire to upset him or cause offence, but if something wasn't done there would soon be a corpse to deal with, and as the ambassador had the nineteenth-century equivalent of diplomatic immunity he would simply leave the country. There was also the problem that all the other guests had spoken privately to Pembroke to say that they would not shoot at all the next day if the ambassador were allowed to take part. Then Pembroke had a brainwave. The ambassador had been admiring a great bustard in a glass case in the hall. It was one of the last of the species to be shot in the south of England – the species was officially extinct locally – and had been in the family for nearly a century. Lord Pembroke didn't mention this to the ambassador, but instead invited him to a bustard shoot on the following day. It was the perfect time of year and bustards were in season, explained his Lordship. But there was one proviso – to have any chance of success the bustard shooter had to shoot alone.

The ambassador took the bait and his excitement knew no bounds. It is not difficult to imagine either that Lord Pembroke would have explained that only the very best shots had any chance of success with this most difficult of birds.

Thus it was that next morning a proud ambassador was lifted on to a pack pony and directed towards Salisbury Plain some miles distant. The other guns waved him off and wished him success and no doubt breathed a collective sigh of relief.

Pembroke and his friends enjoyed an excellent and injury-free day's shooting before returning to the house as the light faded. The ambassador, furious, was at the house already, pacing up and down biting his nails and mumbling to himself.

'I have had a dreadful day,' he exclaimed. 'I have walked miles across foul empty countryside and what do I have to show for it – just three of these damned bustards of yours!'

SHOOTING FROM THE TRAIN

ENGLAND, 1870

An eccentric Victorian nobleman and landowner was very keen on shooting but hated all the walking involved between drives. The problem was particularly acute on his estate as the drives were some distance from each other. He tried travelling by horse; he even tried paying four of his servants extra for carrying him round in a sedan chair. This was fine but it was difficult to shoot from the chair itself, which was what he really wanted, so the experiment was abandoned. Horses tended to bolt at the first bang.

Early bicycles seemed to hold out the prospect of shoot travel of the highest order, but by the time he'd ordered one of the newfangled – and very expensive – machines the duke realised that it would be little use over rough terrain, needing smooth tarmac to work properly.

The duke's hatred of travel meant that, when bicycles and horses and sedan chairs failed, he tried all sorts of schemes to ensure that rather than his having to travel to the birds the birds would travel to him.

He planted woods near the house and had the pheasants driven towards the terrace where he would sit ready to shoot. He even thought that if it worked well he would sit inside the house by the drawing room window and shoot the birds as they flew over.

The crafty old pheasants were too clever to fall for that one. Most simply ran across the lawns and round the house, until

69

the duke spent a fortune erecting a special fence that the birds could neither run round nor hop over. The plan was that as the birds were driven towards the fence they would realise they were about to be trapped if they did not fly. Once airborne they would fly over the house and the duke's sport was assured. That, at least, was the theory.

On the first day the fence driving system was tried the birds flew up all right, but as soon as they saw the house they turned and flew back towards their home wood over the heads of the beaters. The duke could have gone round behind the beaters and caught the birds on their way back but he was determined to find a way to shoot them his way, if not from inside the house then at least from the terrace.

Eventually he had a brainwave. If the pheasants wouldn't come to his seat he would take his seat to the birds. He called in the leading surveyors and engineers and his Grace had a miniature railway built complete with open carriages. He learned to drive the train and persuaded the bemused engineers to build the track so it ran from one drive to the next, even taking in odd bits of woodland on the edges of the estate that were driven only now and then. The result was a great success. The duke had little branch lines built so he could drive in and out of dead ends and he made sure that ultimately if he went far enough on his railway he would get back to where he started. He built other branch lines off the main circuit so he could examine his pens.

After the railway had been completed the great day arrived – the first day of the shooting season. His Grace went down to the platform at the front of the house and boarded his little train. At the first drive he shot as he'd always wished from a specially built seat at the back of the engine. He did very well and enjoyed good sport at all the subsequent drives. He wrote to his friends and invited them to come and try his new shoot. They came and were each accommodated in a small, individual carriage that was then attached to the engine where the duke himself always sat. It was, as he was to observe on many occasions, the triumph of science over nature.

A MAN OBSESSED

YORKSHIRE, 1872

Thomas, the 6th Lord Walsingham (1843-1919) was one of those extraordinary nineteenth-century shots who, excited by the newly introduced breech-loading shotgun, turned a sport into an obsession. There is no doubt that the more he shot – and he shot an enormous amount – the better he became at it until he rivalled that other contender for the title greatest shot ever, Lord de Grey, and it is a curious coincidence that before he succeeded to the title Walsingham, he was plain Tommy de Grey.

Inevitably the two men were often confused, but both were phenomenal shots. Walsingham's greatest day – or most infamous if we judge by modern standards – came when he accounted for more than a thousand grouse at Blubberhouse Moor in Yorkshire.

One reason he was able to do this was that Blubberhouse is shaped roughly like an hour glass and Walsingham positioned himself in the narrowest part, through which inevitably virtually every bird on the moor was channelled, but there is no doubt that shooting at the rate required, his barrels would have been so hot they would have taken the skin off his hands if he'd touched them without gloves.

Again at Blubberhouse Moor on another day in August 1872 he shot precisely 842 grouse and one teal.

Lord de Grey always gave pride of place among the great shots to Walsingham, but a great deal of this had to do with the speed with which Walsingham was able to shoot. On both days at Blubberhouse Walsingham used his own gun – a breech-loader – but even with muzzle-loaders he was an incredibly quick shot although he had to use three guns and two skilled loaders.

Walsingham's skill at rapid shooting only once got the better of him. He was using two loaders and enjoying a day's pheasant shooting. In order to achieve his phenomenal rate of fire he usually used the same two loaders who were actually far more important to the whole shooting machine, as it were, than Walsingham himself. De Grey himself commented on the machinelike precision involved in this kind of team shooting because the least mistiming could throw the whole system into confusion.

The system was that as Walsingham was putting one gun up and firing, one loader was setting the hammers on the second gun. While he did this, the second loader would put shot, wadding and powder into the gun that had just been fired and thus it was a continual round of gun passing and gun firing. Each man had to have the thing timed to perfection and the system of passing – which hand, left or right would give the gun, which hand would take it, and so on – had to be agreed beforehand and rigidly adhered to.

On the day in question all went well and the guns were moving back and forth like pistons on a steam train. The gun barrels would have been far too hot to touch with the naked hand and black powder, the forerunner of modern nitro powders, would have been used. Black powder was much slower burning than modern powders; it also produced huge amounts of dense smoke and on a day when the air is heavy and still, shooting with one black-powder gun, let alone two, can be difficult as it's impossible to see anything for some time after you've fired.

Walsingham and de Grey found themselves in adjacent positions on a pheasant drive. Inevitably smoke filled the air and there was a less than normally efficient loading team in action with Walsingham. Suddenly there was flash and a dense cloud of smoke ascended from Walsingham who, to the eyes of de Grey, looked as if he was on fire, which, in fact, he was. Walsingham carried on exchanging guns and firing despite being on fire, so absorbed was he in the business of bringing down the birds. The loaders stopped loading as they'd been singed and it was only then that Walsingham realised that after a loader had spilled a large amount of black powder, the butt of one of his guns had been burned together with his eyebrows and some of his hair and clothing. Once the mess had been sorted out Walsingham simply carried on shooting.

WOODEN PHEASANTS

YORKSHIRE, ENGLAND, 1873

Charles Waterton turned his Yorkshire estate into an early wildlife sanctuary – probably the first in the world. He built a high wall ten miles round his estate to keep his animals in and poachers out. Unfortunately, despite the time and money spent on these precautions, Waterton noticed telltale signs that poachers were climbing in and shooting the animals and birds he was trying to protect.

He couldn't afford to increase the height of his wall so all over the wood he nailed up wooden silhouettes of birds roosting in the trees. Knowing that even the most daring poacher would not come on to his land during daylight hours he climbed to the top of his favourite tree one night soon after the hundreds of silhouettes had been put up and waited to see what would happen. All through the night he heard occasional gunshots followed, he imagined, by curses as the poachers discovered their mistake and that no birds fell from the trees. But his loud chuckles attracted attention and he is said to have had to leap for his life as an angry poacher, hearing his laughter in the pitch-black night, fired a random shot into the trees and nearly bagged Waterton himself.

BLUNT KEEPER

IRELAND, 1874

Keepers and beaters were not always entirely under the thumb of their masters. Even a great Lord or a member of the royal family might be spoken to by a gillie, a loader, a keeper or a beater in a way that would bring instant dismissal to another servant.

The most famous example of this sort of thing is John Brown, the gillie at Balmoral who became Queen Victoria's most trusted advisor and friend. He regularly spoke to her as if she were an annoying child and he was quite happy to do it in front of other members of her circle. Gasps of horror from her courtiers were ignored by the queen who apparently said, 'He is quite right to upbraid me you know.'

Lord Rossmore, a wealthy Victorian who owned vast acres in various parts of the British Isles, occasionally had to accept that he couldn't always do quite what he wanted to do, but his servants knew that if they wanted change they had to be crafty.

On one famous occasion Rossmore employed a particularly dour Scottish keeper on his estate in Ireland. Whether the Irish beaters took exception to the keeper's depressing Presbyterianism or simply disagreed with his way of managing the shoot is not recorded, but it is certain that the beaters decided that whatever Rossmore thought about the keeper they didn't like him and they were going to be rid of him.

The beaters waited to hatch their plan until Lord Rossmore had invited a particularly distinguished party of guns including several dukes. On the morning of this most prestigious shoot and after a delightful breakfast, the guns made their way to the butts on what Rossmore knew was his best bit of moor. The air would be teeming with good, hard-flying birds – or so he thought. Ten minutes after the first drive began Lord Connaught and the other guns noticed that not a single bird had come their way, yet just a quarter of a mile away across the heather they could see grouse streaming away over completely empty butts.

Moments later the beaters with their distinctive flags came into view having done a splendid job, but in the wrong place.

The beaters were among the most experienced in Ireland and they had worked for Rossmore for many years. They knew the ground better than he did so how on earth had they made such a terrible mistake? The answer must be that the keeper was incompetent, or lazy or worse. He had to go. And he did.

THE DEER FIGHTS BACK

SCOTLAND, 1876

Stalking – or shooting deer with a rifle – has if anything an even more aristocratic pedigree than pheasant or grouse shooting. It's always referred to as stalking to emphasise that shooting the animal is not the point of the thing. Squeezing the trigger is the easy bit. The art of stalking is to use fieldcraft to get close enough to achieve a clean shot. To do that takes real skill, for deer, particularly red deer in the Highlands, can pick up human scent half a mile away.

Charles St John was an enormously experienced stalker who brought many a superb stag down from the hills, but he almost met his match one day in 1876.

He'd spent nearly two hours crawling and slithering quite literally on his stomach towards a particularly fine stag. At last he knew he was close enough to take a shot. Inch by inch, he pushed his rifle over the grassy bank behind which he'd been hiding while he steadied his nerves and calmed his breathing. He looked carefully along the barrel of his rifle. He could see only the stag's horns, but the beast was within easy shot.

St John was afraid to move higher up the burn where he could have seen the whole of the stag's body because the direction of the wind made that highly dangerous. There was no choice. He'd either have to abandon the attempt or take this most difficult of shots.

He took a deep breath and screwed up his nerves; then with his cocked rifle at his shoulder and his finger on the trigger, he kicked a stone, which splashed into the burn that passed close by. The stag started up instantly exposing only its front, but he was very near, scarcely fifty yards. St John broke the habit of a lifetime and took what he knew was by no means a safe and certain shot. He fired. The stag went down, but was up again in a moment and went staggering across the hill.

Although the deer rushed on at a mad pace, St John quickly realised it had been hit and was weakening. As St John watched it swerved, turned back to the burn and came headlong down to within ten yards of him. Then, without warning, the stag tumbled into the water, apparently dead. Feeling confident, St John threw down his rifle and went up to the stag. He grasped its horns ready to heave it from the stream when, without warning, the stag sprang up, flinging him back on the stones. St John hit his head so hard that for a few moments he was unconscious.

Behind him was a steep bank eight or nine feet tall, before him the stag, by now enraged and levelling his horns at the unarmed man. The stag had also managed to cut St John off from his rifle. In desperation he tried to run around the stag, but the beast charged and would have reached him if it had not stumbled again. Once again they stood silently facing each other, the stag glaring and ready to charge, St John immobile and terrified.

Minutes passed and now and again the wounded stag tossed his head with an angry snort. St John knew he had to do something so he took the greatest risk of his life. He jumped out of the burn so suddenly that the stag, momentarily confused, did not follow. From the bank above, St John threw his tartan rug over the stag's head and then threw himself on to it.

He later told friends that he would never be able to account for the stupidity of his actions, but that one rash act nearly cost him his life.

By this time St John felt more sorry for the stag than for himself. Indeed he felt ashamed at what a mess he had made of the whole thing. The poor beast struggled desperately, bucking and whirling with St John hanging on grimly. At last St John was thrown from his back and passed out. Later when he awoke, he checked his wounds, which by sheer luck were not too serious, and found the stag dead just fifty yards away at the edge of the loch.

AGAINST THE REGULATIONS

NORFOLK, 1877

There was an ancient pub on the Norfolk coast called the Cockle, which closed in 1899. It probably closed because the authorities thought – quite rightly – that it was a haunt of smugglers and other undesirables including, inevitably, poachers. But the closure of the Cockle was a sad day for many a professional wildfowler, including a remarkable character called Mr Capps.

Capps was a man who shot geese and duck for a living and he did it pretty much from one end of the country to the other. No one ever quite knew how he travelled between the northern firths, the Wash and the Norfolk coast, since he never appeared to have any money, but he was a regular at the Cockle where, on arrival, he would look about him for friends and acquaintances. If he saw anyone he knew, he would whip out his hip flask and insist on adding a drop of his own concoction to whatever they were already drinking.

Capps's name became legendary after an incident one day in the 1870s. It was at a time when Norfolk was subject to occasional invasions of sand grouse – an oriental visitor that caused a bit of a storm locally as naturalists and bird watchers from all over the country came down to Norfolk to catch a glimpse of these rare and unusual birds. Collectors were much more interested in bagging a couple to be stuffed and added to their collections. A friend, who collected birds and their eggs, asked Capps to see if he could bag a couple of sand grouse for his collection. Normally Capps would not have dreamed of trying to shoot these birds as they'd virtually been wiped out by local gunners and it was out of season anyway. But his friend was persuasive and offered Capps a good sum for bagging the birds, so Capps set off early one morning in his punt. He was not the sort of man to be embarrassed even when he was breaking the law so he was quite open about what he was up to and had spoken openly of it in the Cockle the night before. By mid-morning everyone round about knew of Capps' expedition, including Mr Banks the village bobby, who decided to arrest Capps as soon as he came ashore.

Banks knew that Capps would eventually come to the Cockle Inn or into the village so he called in for a drink to await the arrival of the sand grouse gunner. The landlord knew that trouble was brewing and he didn't want Capps arrested on the premises – partly because it would be bad for business and partly because he liked Capps, who was a good customer. So he sent his wife out the back door and down to the beach half a mile away where Capps was sure to come ashore. She was to warn him and persuade him to give her the birds while he carried on up the creek into the village and the Cockle Inn.

Capps would have none of this. He'd bagged a couple of sand grouse and he was proud of it. He paddled up the creek, tied up and walked straight into the Cockle with the sand grouse swinging from his hand. The village bobby was sitting reading a newspaper and had a half-empty tankard of beer in front of him.

Capps threw the birds down in front of the constable who spluttered out: 'Do you know that these are sand grouse and that it is illegal to shoot them?'

Before he could say another word Capps bellowed out, 'Do you know it is against regulations to be drinking in a public house in a policeman's uniform while on duty?' With that Capps escorted the policeman into the street and shut the door behind him.

An old wildfowler sitting in a dark corner of the Cockle heard the whole thing and related the story with glee until his dying day. He also explained how, on coming back into the Cockle after removing the policeman, Capps had come over to him and said: 'Let that be a lesson to you. Don't drink out of hours and don't shoot out of season.'

The old wildfowler was even more amused by this as he'd been committing both offences day in and day out for years.

INDESCRIBABLE CHAOS

GERMANY, 1877

When the church still had a great deal of political power, churchmen liked to join the powerful in their sports and pastimes. This could lead to enormous problems because the rich felt that the clergy could not be easily criticised, which meant greedy or trigger-happy prelates spoiling the shoot for others.

In Germany a famous churchman, the Abbot of Tepl, owned and managed vast acres around the town of Marienbad, and he was keen to attract English sportsmen to the estate. He knew that the trick was to persuade the future king to come over, for where the Prince of Wales went the English aristocracy was sure to follow. The Prince of Wales eventually did reach Marienbad, lured as much as anything by the extraordinary lunches that were a feature of the estate.

The estate was famous for its vast numbers of birds, particularly partridges, and the abbot ensured that when the future king arrived, there were even more birds than usual – the hapless birds were brought in by train in hundreds of specially built cages to augment the tens of thousands already on the ground.

On the Prince of Wales's first day in the field lunch started before any of the drives. This was to allow enough time for the guests to work their way through the vast pile of food which was brought out in relay after relay by dozens of domestic servants.

Elderly clerics tried to marshal the hundreds of beaters and flagmen, many of whom had turned up uninvited, and at one stage (as the feast neared its end sometime in the late afternoon) it seemed that there were more people milling about than birds. The situation worsened when hundreds of spectators, hearing that the Prince of Wales was nearby, left their houses and wandered all over the shoot.

Those elderly monks – they were all over seventy – who had not been given any organising duties came out with ancient guns of every description to take part in the shoot and the scene was described by one observer as indescribably chaotic.

One monk was stopped by a member of the future king's entourage and asked where he planned to shoot.

'I will be walking with the beaters. It is safe yes. I am well to the back and will be perfectly safe and accurate unless of course someone shoots at me – if they are so unwise I can let you know I will shoot straight back!'

The crowds grew ever larger as the day wore on, yet still the courses arrived one after another at the luncheon tables and the guests grew increasingly heavy and sleepy and less inclined to move. By this time spectators, amateur flagmen and beaters were swarming everywhere.

Then at last the moment had arrived. The guests, including the now hugely bloated prince, were helped up from the table and escorted to their butts, many of which had been specially built for the occasion. Then in some vague, perhaps almost instinctive way, the great swarms of beaters moved off like birds on migration and the fun – in theory at least – began.

The prince was placed in a particularly magnificent butt and the first thing he saw ahead of him and to either side were two huge kites that had been launched earlier in the day. At the end of each kite string was a small boy – both boys looked in continual danger of being towed away by their charges. The idea of the kites, one assumes, was that they were somehow meant to concentrate as many partridges as possible over the future king. Inevitably, perhaps, they actually helped keep the birds on the ground. Huge numbers of partridges were reported as coming towards the guns, but it was only when they reached them that it was discovered they were still on the ground – everywhere the prince looked, partridges were mingling with the crowds of spectators. Hardly a bird flew that day and the guns and spectators were probably equally astonished to hear that the total bag for the day – according to the Abbot of Tepl who'd organised the whole thing – was 36 brace. It was later discovered that this low but respectable figure had been achieved by counting all the partridges that had died in the train, flown into trees or were caught by the dogs.

The Prince of Wales's reaction to this extraordinary day is not recorded but he had a sense of humour and must certainly have revelled in the eccentricity of the whole thing.

PLAYING DEAD

IRELAND, 1877

A boy out shooting in County Westmeath, Ireland, in the 1870s stood at the edge of the uncut section of hay in a field where the mowers were still busy at work. He had shot a couple of rabbits and had hopes that he would be able to take home a pheasant or two when suddenly out of the hay ran a bright brown bird. The boy lifted his gun to fire and then realised he had not reloaded after his earlier shots, so without thinking he set off in pursuit of the bird, which was busily running across the cut hay. Seconds later he saw the bird keel over. The boy picked the bird up and carried it home. His mother told him it was a corncrake and she laid it on the kitchen table. The boy did not tell her that it had simply dropped dead when he chased it, fearing she would simply not believe him. He was very proud of the bird, however, and as his mother bustled around the kitchen he couldn't help gazing admiringly at it. For a second he was sure he saw its eye open, but it couldn't have and he dismissed the idea. When it happened again he called out to his mother, but on hearing his voice the bird seemed immediately to shut its eye again. Mother and son placed the still apparently dead bird where they could see it more easily and stared at it, keeping quite still. A minute later the eye opened, the bird leaped to its feet and legged it out the open door with the young man and his mother in hot pursuit. Once in the garden the bird took to the air and was never seen again.

DOG WRESTLING

ALBANIA, 1880

According to William Bagot whose *Guide to Shooting* appeared in 1887, European shooting dogs were not quite up to the standard of their English counterparts. On the face of it this might have seemed to be the Englishman's simple preference for the familiar, but some of Bagot's descriptions of Albanian shooting dogs suggest otherwise.

He describes an incident in the Balkans when an Englishman out shooting with a team of Albanian guides was attacked by one of their dogs – a massive black Alsatian with a reputation for savagery. The Englishman weighed over sixteen stone and was a noted rugby player, rower, boxer and all-round sportsman. In fear of his life he grabbed the attacking animal in midair, twisted it and snapped its neck. It died instantly. Now, the Englishman had been warned to stay on the right side of his Albanian guides, as their reputation was none too savoury. It was said that in their home regions they thrived on family feuds that lasted for generations and they would always avenge a slight or an insult no matter what the circumstances. And vengeance always meant death. But if these wild mountain men were passionate about defending their honour they were said to be even more passionate about their dogs – Bagot said that shooters were warned to take particular care never to wound or injure an Albanian's dog in any way.

So our intrepid Englishman, out shooting with his Albanian guides in that remote area of Europe and with one of their dogs dead at his feet must have thought his time was up. But not a bit of it. The dog's owner stood open-mouthed at the scene for a few icy moments then clapped the Englishman on the back, congratulated him on an extraordinary deed and presented him with a beautifully inlaid dagger.

Back in London several months later the Englishman discovered that the dagger had been specially made some years earlier for the King of Greece. It had never been reported missing and how it had come into the possession of that Albanian peasant has never been discovered.

NINCOMPOOPS

AUSTRIA, 1880

So far as the Englishman is concerned all foreign shots are at best nincompoops, at worst dangerous incompetents. At driven pheasant shoots Americans are said to get overexcited which makes them shoot at everything even if the birds are so close that they are turned instantly to pâté. Rich young men from the Middle East, a little unsure as to the etiquette of grouse shooting turn up with machine guns, Germans shoot deer running and don't give a damn how many they injure. And so on.

Occasionally the myths turn into reality as they did for two Austrian aristocrats out stag shooting one crisp morning in 1880.

Prince Hohenloe and Baron Veitinghoff had often shot together without mishap and they were the best of friends. On the day in question they agreed to decoy the stags using a call made by blowing a small, specially made horn. When they reached the area where they expected to find the stags they separated, agreeing to meet later for lunch.

As the hours wore on with not a single shot from either man they unknowingly got rather close to each other – dangerously close as it turned out.

Being so close each heard the other's stag call and believed that he was about to get a shot at a superb beast. Each man began to imitate the heavy tread that a stag would expect to hear from a rival and that, combined with the two highly realistic calls, brought the two men to within thirty feet of each other without either having the least intimation that he'd made a dreadful mistake.

The undergrowth was so thick that neither man could see a thing. Each man waited, calling an occasional challenge note on his horn. Each was convinced that nearby stood a shootable stag.

Finally the prince, tired of waiting, fired three times in quick succession roughly in the direction in which his supposed quarry was standing. The first bullet ricocheted off the baron's cartridge belt; the second hit his solid gold watch and the third buried itself deeply but harmlessly in a pocket book stuffed thick with papers. The baron was completely unscathed and remained convinced that a stag was just in front of him. He'd heard the three shots but thought a few of his cartridges had accidentally exploded and was in the process of throwing his cartridge belt to the ground when the prince appeared before him.

Both men were to dine out on the story of the baron's extraordinary good luck for many years after, but they declined ever to shoot stags together again.

IN PURSUIT OF SEALS

SCOTLAND, 1880

The year 1900 seems to mark a shift in some attitudes towards shooting. The certain belief that animals were entirely designed to be used for any purpose by man had moved a little closer to the contemporary idea that animals too have rights. Thus more sportsmen began to look back with nostalgia and some regret at the days of their youth when, almost without thinking, they hunted and shot everything that came within range.

Anthony Gathorne-Hardy had shot one example at least of every wild animal in the U.K., but looking back in old age when he wrote and published his memoirs a little before Queen Victoria died, he always remembered an extraordinary day when, off the coast of Argyllshire, he went seal shooting. He shot seals for their pelts, which were once popular as rugs or wall hangings. Like tiger-skin rugs sealskin is now, of course, a natural resource that we do not like to harvest.

On the day in question Gathorne-Hardy set off from his remote house by dogcart with his sister in attendance and two friends who were golfing fanatics.

Gathorne-Hardy had studied the business of shooting seals and knew that even the slightest mishit would mean the loss of the much-coveted pelt because an injured seal would, with one kick, get down into deep water and never surface again.

After crossing a good deal of sand and rock at an absolute snail's pace, Gathorne-Hardy had to wade through five feet of

91

treacherous seawater to cross a dangerous channel. He then had to lie on his belly for a half-mile wriggle across the sort of sharp rock that leaves you scratched and bruised, but he was a determined man and in true sportsman style he would have argued that the sport of seal hunting, the real skill of the thing, consisted in this long, slow approach to get within range.

After two hours of muscle-cramping manoeuvres he peered above a rock and saw a group of half a dozen or so grey seals basking in the sea fifty yards out from a rocky outcrop. They were certainly within range of his gun. By this time Gathorne-Hardy's clothes were soaked through and torn in places. He'd only managed to keep his rifle dry by carrying it slightly above his head commando style.

His first shot produced a tiny splash where a seal's head had been.

Terrified that he might lose this seal – if indeed he'd even hit it – Gathorne-Hardy threw down his rifle and raced through the surf before diving head first into the icy water. He swam to the spot where he'd last seen the seal, arriving just in time to grab its flippers as they began to sink. Kicking and tugging furiously Gathorne-Hardy was just able to keep the seal afloat and move it towards the shore – but only just.

With each pull towards the shore he felt the weight of the dead seal pull him down. Then he spotted a small, rocky outcrop barely the size of a dinner table and just managed to wedge the seal against it while he removed his big shooting boots and tied them round his neck. He then set off again with the seal in tow towards the shore. Just a few yards into the journey his boots slipped from his neck and down into the deep water never to be seen again.

Gathorne-Hardy swam the few yards back to the dinner-table rock and left the seal wedged there. He returned alone to the shore and, leaving the water, crossed the rocks, cutting his feet badly in the process.

Soaked and bootless, Gathorne-Hardy ran two miles across the rough stony ground into the hills. Here at an isolated crofter's cottage he banged on the door. The woman of the house looked out of the window suspiciously at this bedraggled figure, but Scottish hospitality being what it is she opened the door and asked if he would like a drink and something to eat. Breathless, and no doubt seeming decidedly eccentric, Gathorne-Hardy in clipped Etonian accents asked the woman for a rope. All she had were a few tattered bits of rough, home-made cord which he was able to tie together before making the mad dash two miles back to the beach, his feet now steaming blood.

Back at the shore he saw his seal's flippers still just sticking out of the water by the dining-table rock. He swam out as quickly as he could, tied the rope round the flippers and began again the interminable tow towards the shore. Halfway there the old bits of rope broke and the seal sank into deep water – too deep for diving.

Like most Victorian sportsmen, Gathorne-Hardy just didn't know when to give up. Despite near exhaustion and badly injured feet, he returned at first light next day with an armful of grappling hooks and several hundred yards of new rope. By now the weather had changed and a storm was raging, but Gathorne-Hardy spent the day in what was eventually to prove a completely fruitless search for the seal.

PORTUGUESE TERROR

ENGLAND, 1881

Go shooting anywhere in Britain today and you are more likely
to be judged on your manners and attitude to safety than on
your ability to knock things out of the sky. Even the rich, the
famous and the aristocratic – perhaps even royalty – expect to
be judged in this way, but it was not always thus. And certainly
not for foreign dignitaries. The problem with foreigners was
not that they were foreign – it was that they were used to
shooting in countries where things were not done as in Britain
and shooting is not the same the world over. Different
traditions make shooting in two apparently similar countries as
different as chalk and cheese. Coming to England and saying
you can shoot because you grew up shooting in Portugal,
Greece or wherever is meaningless, yet still the invitations went
out and then there was the problem of how to be polite to a
guest while ensuring that he did not kill anyone during his stay.
The problem was a recurring one throughout Britain in the
nineteenth century, but particularly on aristocratic estates
where the owners – like the British royal family – were
frequently related to German or Russian families.

Lady Cardigan married a Portuguese nobleman and in her
memoirs, written in old age and long after her husband was
dead, she describes the terror she felt whenever he invited his
friends to England to shoot. With a gun in their hands these
otherwise civilised Europeans became a cross between
uncontrollable children and Wild West cowboys. Once armed

and in the field they shot at everything that moved, including each other, and it is a continuing source of wonder that more people were not killed. Lady Cardigan's solution – she claims – was to get the servants to remove the shot from the cartridges to be used next day and replace it with bran. Frustrated by the fact that they never seemed to hit anything (bran not being quite as good as lead) her husband's guests probably fired even more wildly than usual, but at least they could do no more harm.

NOTORIOUS GOSSIP

SCOTLAND, 1882

Practical jokes – so long as they don't involve messing around with guns – have always been popular among those who shoot and many a dull day's shooting has been enlivened by an incident that will keep it in the memory of every participant for many years to come.

Two Scottish shooters were very keen drinking men, but they weren't too happy when they discovered that a local woman – the wife of a keeper on another estate – had been gossiping about their liking for a dram or two. There was nothing they could do about it but bide their time, which is exactly what they did. Then one day, returning from a shoot in the back of the game cart, they had a moment of inspiration – or rather one of them did, for the other had passed out from drinking too much. The slightly more sober man made his unconscious companion comfortable, but in a position in which his head was just a few inches below the level of the boards at the side of the cart. If the drunken man lifted his head just six inches anyone the carriage passed by would be able to see it. The more sober fellow directed the cart deliberately on a bit of a detour so it would pass the house of the notorious gossip. Luck was with him, for as they passed the cottage the woman was in the garden and as she heard the horses' hooves she looked up quickly and turned towards the sound.

As she started to speak the more sober of the two friends in the cart lifted his unconscious friend's head up by the hair and shouted: 'I have a man's head here.' The woman screamed and fled back into her house.

'That'll give her something to gossip about,' said the man in the game cart.

SHOT TO EXTINCTION

CAUCASUS, RUSSIA, 1882

George Littledale may well have been the last man to shoot the now extinct aurochs. This huge relative of the American bison once roamed across vast areas of central Europe and Russia, but the incursions of man gradually destroyed its forest habitat and it had been hunted to the brink of extinction by the end of the nineteenth century.

In the early 1880s Littledale was asked to obtain an aurochs specimen for the British Museum. Curiously the museum wanted the specimen precisely because the poor old aurochs was known to be down to a few dozen individuals at most. The museum wanted a specimen or two before it was too late and it never seems to have occurred to the museum, nor indeed to Littledale, that in shooting a specimen for the museum he was contributing to the certainty of the aurochs' disappearance.

The aurochs was already so rare that Littledale spent several years just trying to come across a sign of the animal. He employed numerous elderly hunters in the Caucasus region of Russia, but to no avail.

During each of his trips to the region Littledale managed to shoot plenty of small game, but the aurochs eluded him again and again. He himself admitted that most people in the 1880s were convinced that the aurochs was already extinct.

The turning point came when a Russian hunter – one of Littledale's party – explained that he would never get within range of an aurochs unless he washed his rifle each morning in the water from at least three different streams. And the water had to be collected at dawn or only a little after to make sure that the water for the rifle was taken before either man or beast had drunk from the stream.

Littledale later explained how he dismissed the idea as nonsense but thought it might be worth going through the motions for psychological reasons – it might have a beneficial effect on the mood of his local guides who were certain it would improve his luck.

Next day he got up at dawn, washed his rifle in three streams, and later that morning found the tracks of what the local men were sure was an aurochs. Three hours later Littledale shot it, together with a female. Both were duly sent to the British Museum and later transferred to the Natural History Museum where they remain to this day. The aurochs has been officially extinct since about 1910.

INVISIBLE BIRD

ENGLAND, 1884

The Duke of Devonshire owned one of the best shooting estates in Britain but was also one of the worst shots in the country. His haphazard ways were legendary, but what he lacked in skill he made up for in enthusiasm. In a career of incompetence that lasted many years he probably established the record (though no one was counting) for the greatest number of cartridges fired by any man at absolutely nothing, but occasionally he surpassed even his own consistent level of hopelessness. With one shot he once hit a pheasant, the dog that was chasing it, the dog's owner and his own chef. He wasn't in the least perturbed, expressing concern only that his lunch might not be quite up to its usual standard if the chef were incapacitated.

In the same year while shooting at Creswell Crags he fired both barrels in quick succession and toppled a very high partridge. His friends were so impressed that they let out a cheer. At the end of the drive his Lordship asked, 'Why was I cheered for missing that pheasant with both barrels?'

'But my Lord,' came the reply, 'you hit a magnificently high partridge.'

'Good Lord,' the duke is said to have replied, 'I was trying for a pheasant. I didn't even see that partridge.'

So keen was the duke to gain some belated reputation as a half-decent shot that he asked that the incident not be mentioned again. Of course this was never likely to happen and within days the story was everywhere and the drive was known forever after as Hartington's Stand (Devonshire had yet to inherit his dukedom and was still plain Lord Hartington).

MAD IN THE ZOO

LONDON, 1884

One of the biggest game animals shot in England – in an adventure that rivals anything one might read in a *Boy's Own* annual – was shot right in the centre of London at the end of the nineteenth century.

An elephant destined for a private zoo suddenly went mad and killed its keeper before escaping and damaging a railway locomotive, besides smashing several stables and outhouses.

The animal had recently arrived from India and the team who came to meet him and escort him from his specially built railway carriage had been assured that he was enormously well behaved and would therefore be ideal for the captive breeding programme that the zoo had planned. But once out of his carriage the elephant decided he did not like the look of his new surroundings. After a two-hour-long session during which the elephant smashed everything in sight it was cornered in a railway siding where it could neither escape nor do much more damage.

The authorities, too terrified to take any more risks and this being long before tranquilliser darts, decided to call in a horse slaughterer. He took one look at the animal, made his excuses and left without saying a word, other than that he knew a gunmaker who he would have a word with. The horse slaughterer promised the gunmaker that he would give him five pounds for shooting the elephant so long as he, the slaughterer, could have the carcase. The gunmaker agreed, but on condition that he could have the teeth, the tusks, the two front teeth and the tail. They eventually agreed the bargain and the gunmaker went off to his storeroom to find a suitably heavy weapon. They set off together towards the railway goods yard. 'What do you want with the carcase?' said the gunmaker.

'Perfect for the cat's meat man,' came the reply.

They walked the rest of the way in silence.

The gunmaker had with him a .577 elephant rifle that fired nickel bullets with ninety grams of cordite – a mighty weapon by any standards.

When the two men reached the goods yard the elephant was dragging round a steamroller that had been attached to its leg via a massive but rather rusty chain. The thick wooden walls of the yard were being regularly battered by the elephant and looked like they might soon give way. When the elephant saw the two new arrivals he grew even more enraged. The situation was made more difficult by the fact that the elephant kept rearing up on its hind legs. A shot taken at that level might mean a bullet whizzing past the animal's head and then on for about a mile across London where who knows who it would hit. The gunmaker was a little concerned too that when he did fire the gun the massive report would stop the traffic and make people for miles about assume that a gas main had exploded or that a foreign power had launched a surprise attack on the British capital. Nerving himself and staying as calm as possible, the gunmaker waited his moment and then quickly fired. The elephant keeled over as quiet as a mouse and that was the end of that – apart from the fact that the shot had severed the poor animal's jugular vein and the whole yard was now awash in about a foot of blood.

The gunmaker kept the tusks and displayed them proudly in his shop in the city until German bombs flattened the whole street during the Second World War.

BEAR SACRIFICE

NORTH AMERICA, 1884

Shooting in British Columbia in 1920, Frantz Rosenberg always took North American Indian trackers with him. They had an almost intuitive ability to sense the presence of game and then to bring him within shot of it. As they made camp one night one of the trackers told Rosenberg an extraordinary story from his childhood.

There had been several terrible winters in North America during the last decade of the nineteenth century when the tracker was a boy. During one particularly savage December, the tribe to which the tracker belonged was camped on the Stickine River. Their winter hunt had failed almost completely and there was a very real danger that many of the women and children would die of starvation – they simply had no stores of food. The once great herds of buffalo and caribou that for so long had sustained them were gone, all but wiped out by European settlers who shot them by the thousand from passing trains just for the fun of it.

At the edge of despair the tribal elders decided to send one of their strongest hunters to scout around the area and see if he could find anything. The hunter wandered for miles, up higher and higher into the forest and without warning, as he later told the tale, he found himself confronted by a huge grizzly bear. Even if he managed to shoot it before it got to him the hunter knew that he would never be able to carry the meat back down to the tribe, but then something strange happened.

The bear showed no signs of aggression and began instead to walk around the hunter down towards the river. The hunter followed until the bear came close to the camp. Only then did he kill the bear. Then there was enough meat for all and the tribe was saved. There seemed to be no explanation other than that the bear had sacrificed itself for the tribe.

The tracker who told Rosenberg the story insisted that animals, like men, would sometimes sacrifice themselves in this way.

THE COLONEL'S NOSE

NORFOLK, 1885

The great Sir Ralph Payne Gallwey, one of the best-known shots of the Victorian era, remembered an incident that showed how extraordinarily badly the legal and clerical professions could behave when there was a bit of sport in the offing.

A famously greedy clergyman who was constantly trying to shoot birds that were much closer to the next gun in the line – a grievously unsporting and ungentlemanly thing to do – took a day's shooting with, among others, a young lawyer.

During one drive the lawyer and the clergyman walked, with a number of other guns, up a young plantation, shooting pheasants that rose ahead of them and then tried to double back over their heads. Any birds that flew forward and away from the line of guns were to be the preserve of a very stout, lame, red-nosed and choleric old colonel who was stationed on the distant side of the plantation.

The lawyer was strolling comfortably down a well-cut ride at the other end of which the colonel stood patiently waiting. The lawyer shot several times into the trees above the old colonel's head and, each time he did so, the old colonel roared at the top of his voice.

'Let 'em rise, damn you sir, let 'em rise.'

The lawyer then saw the old colonel pull out an enormous handkerchief and apply it to the end of his nose. The colonel looked down at the handkerchief and began to curse in a most terrifying manner. He laid down his gun and limped behind a tree.

The lawyer realised he had peppered the old man with shot and dreaded the consequences. What was he to do? Then, in an instant, came inspiration.

The clergyman, eager to shoot the lawyer's birds, had been endeavouring to squeeze the lawyer off his ride, for he – the clergyman – was jealous of the lawyer's comfortable position in the open while he had to struggle through thick undergrowth while scarcely getting a shot. He'd continually pleaded with the lawyer to change places with him, but to no avail.

As soon as the lawyer realised that something was wrong with the colonel he offered to change places with the parson. Highly pleased with himself the reverend strolled confidently down the ride and when he reached the end came face to face with the injured colonel who, with his vast handkerchief, was attempting to stem the steady flow of blood from a piece of lead shot that had lodged right in the centre of the tip of his nose.

For a full five minutes the old colonel fired the most indescribable volley of abuse at the open-mouthed clergyman.

The mildest expression he used was, 'You sir, are a damned disgrace to your cloth. A disgrace!' When the poor parson tried to explain that he could not have been the culprit (as indeed he could not) he was told not to make the matter worse by trying to shift the blame on to someone else.

'You damn well shot me sir,' said the colonel, hopping about on his one good leg and mopping continually at his nose. 'You damn well shot me all over – limbs, body and head. You did nothing but shoot straight into me from one end of the ride to the other till you saw I was wounded, and then you would have hit me again had I not run for shelter.'

PRACTICAL JOKER

LINCOLNSHIRE, 1885

It is no exaggeration to say that Sir Ralph Payne Gallwey devoted his life to shooting. He thought of it both as an art and a science and was genuinely bewildered that academics, journalists and men of science were not more interested in it. The title of one of his best-known books reveals something of his seriousness about shooting; *High Pheasants in Theory and Practice* tried to reduce what is essentially a relatively simple form of hunting to a set of basic principles of a kind more in keeping with physics and chemistry. In the field Payne Gallwey was equally serious and in just one year in the early 1890s he travelled a little under 8,000 miles round Britain shooting wildfowl – ducks and geese – wherever he went. His best-known book, which is still occasionally read today, is *Letters to Young Shooters* published in three volumes.

Payne Gallwey was by any standards an eccentric and, though his passion for shooting would be considered unsympathetic and excessive today, any study of the man's character would be amply rewarded. His wit and liking for practical jokes and whimsical flights of fancy were legendary and it is sad that so few of his sallies were recorded.

Two of the best anecdotes about Payne Gallwey concern shooting, if rather indirectly.

He was once heading up to the Wash by train, his gun and cartridge cases spread around him – a common sight at that time on public transport – when a middle-aged woman entered his compartment at a remote Norfolk station. Now Payne Gallwey always liked to make conversation – he could be enormously charming at a time when strangers in railway carriages talked much more readily to each other than they do today.

So Payne Gallwey began to talk about the weather, the state of the railways, the condition of the empire, but as polite as he was and despite the exercise of his great charm the woman remained virtually silent, which meant Payne Gallwey had to suffer the indignity of what he saw as a very boring journey. He decided to make the best of a bad job and tried to sleep, which he did. He woke a little later to discover that the woman had also fallen asleep. When the great shooting man arrived at his station he stepped down on to the platform, but held the door for a moment while his luggage and cases were removed. By this time the woman had woken up and doffing his hat to her Payne Gallwey said, 'Madam, we might not have enjoyed much conversation, but at least we can say we have slept together.' The woman's response is not recorded.

On another occasion Payne Gallwey decided to play a trick on his optician so when he went for an eye test he sneaked a close look at the card he knew he would be expected to read from a distance of ten feet later on. He even memorised the name of the card's printer, which was in absolutely minute print. When he had read the card out to the optician's satisfaction – and no small surprise – he announced, 'Hang on a minute. I think there's a bit more on the card that I can read.'

'I can assure you,' said the astonished optician, 'there is nothing else on the card.'

'But there is,' said Payne Gallwey, who then proceeded to read out the name of the printer.

The optician was so astonished that he tried to make Payne Gallwey the subject of a series of medical experiments for the benefit of world science.

RUDE WORDS

ENGLAND, 1885

For some years it was the custom on a famous shoot in England to dress all the beaters in white smocks of the sort once worn by shepherds and other agricultural workers. Each man's smock had a different letter on the back from A through to Q. The letters were printed in big solid black letters so they could be seen from a distance.

The beaters hated the smocks but the shoot owners felt it made the beaters more visible which was a good thing. Of course it wasn't done so that the guns would be sure to see the beaters in plenty of time to stop shooting. It was more that any pheasant seeing a group of bright white figures approaching would be sure to fly up instantly.

Things continued for a few seasons but grumbles and discontent were increasing on the shoot and the beaters were clearly unhappy. This was in the days when beaters would not have dared even to speak to one of the guns, let alone the shoot owner. Still less would they complain about what they were asked to do – many were estate workers as well as beaters and their jobs would certainly be at stake if they complained about anything.

Then one of the beaters' leaders had an idea. He made sure that each time a group of guns and their wives came out on the lawn for lunch the beaters sitting or standing further off across the lawn just happened to have their backs to the ladies and gentlemen and, quite by chance, the beaters sat in lines that spelled out obscene words. When the words became so gross that the ladies were forced to blush and look the other way it was time to act – quietly the owner of the shoot admitted defeat and the hated smocks disappeared.

THE SWIMMING DOG

SCOTLAND, 1885

Many extraordinary shooting stories concern dogs. This has a great deal to do with the fact that a good shooting dog will work till it is exhausted; but it's also a simple consequence of the fact that for many shooting men a dog is the sole companion for hours spent waiting on some remote headland or abandoned foreshore. In fact, the long and the short of it is that for many shooting men life without a dog is almost unthinkable. This isn't entirely a matter of sentiment either because for certain kinds of shooting a dog is essential.

John Guille Millais, a Victorian writer now long forgotten, seemed at times far more interested in the antics of his shooting dog than in the shooting for which he'd bought the dog in the first place. This passion for all things canine reached dizzying heights after an extraordinary day on the Tay in the winter of 1885. Millais had downed a goose that crashed into the sea. His dog, Jet, set off after it into an icy, roaring sea that most dogs would have refused. In fact, when he sent his dog in Millais didn't think for a minute that it would even attempt the retrieve. But the dog set off through the churning waves as if he were out on the village pond. Millais watched as the dog swam further and further out into the estuary. The dog disappeared but Millais managed to pick it up again using his telescope. Then, even through the telescope, it could no longer be seen. Faced with the prospect of losing his dog Millais sprang into action. He ran a mile or so along the foreshore hoping he would find a boat pulled up somewhere or perhaps a punt gunner working the inshore waters. Nothing. Then after almost a mile he spotted a bait-digger who at first refused to let Millais borrow his boat. In fact, Millais and the bait-digger almost came to blows because the sea was so rough that the bait-digger thought if he let his boat go he would never see it again. Somehow Millais managed to persuade the man and he rowed off through the breaking surf. A good way out in the estuary he shouted and called to the dog but could see little among the waves. Then he spotted a speck in the distance. They were nearly a mile from the shore when he spotted Jet who, in desperate trouble, had refused to let go of the massive goose that he still held in his mouth, despite the fact that he could never have got back to land carrying the bird. When Millais pulled him from the sea Jet was clearly exhausted and about to go under, but it was also clear that he would have died with that goose in his mouth.

So strong were the currents that it took Millais four hours to get back through the racing tides. Jet lived for many years afterwards, but Millais never forgot his bravery and he was heartbroken when he finally died late one night by the fireside.

STONE THROWING

SCOTLAND, 1886

The vast and relatively uninhabited Highland region of Scotland has always been difficult to protect from poachers, but in serious and persistent cases the police and local keepers have been known to wait for days in an attempt to catch the culprits.

On a fine autumn morning in 1886 a team of keepers employed on a Highland estate were out watching the deer on a distant hillside. Through their telescopes the four men had spied a particularly fine stag when suddenly they heard the sharp crack of a rifle. A second later they watched the stag fall dead. The stalker and keepers knew that no one was out legitimately shooting, so this must have been the work of a poacher.

They hunkered down and waited, hoping the poacher would reveal himself. They had no reason to think that the poacher had any idea that he'd been seen. As night came on two keepers hid themselves near the carcase of the deer. The stalker and another estate worker hid in the narrow road that cut through the estate near where the deer had fallen.

There was plenty of moonlight so the waiting men could see pretty clearly. Then in the early hours the poacher appeared on the open ground and advanced towards the deer. Then he did something extraordinary – he began hurling rocks at the stag. One after another the rocks came crashing down around the stag and inevitably a few fell beyond the stag where the two keepers were hiding. Eventually one of the keepers was hit. The shock of the blow made him cry out. As soon as he heard the noise the poacher bolted back the way he'd come. The four keepers immediately set off after him, but after running for a few hundred yards the poacher disappeared into an area of thick shrubbery and trees and his four pursuers soon realised they would never find him. They returned disheartened to the deer thinking that at least they would get the deer the poacher had shot. But when they returned they found the deer had gone. The poacher had actually been a decoy to lure them away and his friends had obviously been watching the watchers until the coast was clear. They then dashed in, took the deer and were long gone by the time the keepers returned. The whole thing, from start to finish, had been a set up.

CROCODILE JUMPING

VENEZUELA, 1887

Lord Waterton was the first of the great conservationists. Although he was a keen shooting man in his youth he soon realised that slaughtering large numbers of animals – or rare animals – just because the modern gun enabled one to do it easily was senseless and immoral. On several occasions he fell out with his Yorkshire neighbours who thought that all animals (except dogs and horses) were legitimate targets, and when one man boasted that he had shot the last raven in Yorkshire Waterton threatened to whip him through the town.

'The man is an impostor and a scoundrel,' Waterton is reported to have said from then on whenever his neighbour's name was mentioned. 'How can he boast and think he has done a fine thing in depriving this part of England of the last individual of an interesting and lively species.'

Other landowners of course would have disagreed, for England was still a place where in the main any wild animal was fair game and in some ways the rarer it was the more shooting men would tend to pursue it. Waterton hated this so he built a high wall some ten miles round his estate. He then put advertisements in all the local papers offering to pay anyone who brought him various animals alive and uninjured. These he released within the great wall of his estate and there they were left unmolested.

Now Waterton may have been a conservationist on his home estate, but he had in his youth a great passion for shooting and

116

adventure. He travelled the world to add animals to his collection. It's true that he liked to keep hares and hedgehogs and other native animals alive and there is no doubt that if he'd been able to transport a live rhino from Africa to Wakefield he would have done so. This was clearly impossible so Waterton shot his rhino and other animals and then brought them home.

His house was awash with stuffed rhinos, with gorillas in huge barrels of pickling fluid, with sun-dried antelope and stuffed platypus. Waterton was so keen on exotic animals that he even used bits from various animals to create bizarre, apparently realistic creatures.

On expeditions to South America to collect more creatures for his collection Waterton would go barefoot everywhere, sleeping at night on the hard ground and living as far as possible by eating the animals he shot. So addicted did he become to this way of life that when he finally returned home for good, he ran about his estate barefoot, even in the depths of winter, rarely wore a coat and slept in a bare attic on the floorboards. He used a thick block of mahogany for a pillow.

His greatest moment came when he was in pursuit of a crocodile. He'd stalked several animals over a period of a week in a South American swamp, but hated the idea of taking a wild shot and injuring an animal. He therefore waited until he could take a really safe shot that would kill the animal instantly. Unfortunately, as luck would have it, the only crocodile he was able to get a really good shot at was a huge thing and, despite all his efforts, Waterton's first bullet only succeeded in injuring it. With a party of beaters he pursued the injured animal, but they could never get quite close enough to capture it. Waterton became exasperated and the next time he got close to the animal he threw aside his gun and leaped on the crocodile's back. As it writhed and thrashed he hung on long enough to pass a rope round the angry animal and the others were then able to drag it ashore. Waterton's reputation for fearlessness and eccentricity stayed with him for the rest of his long life.

RIDING A LION

MABOTSE, AFRICA, 1887

The Victorian era gave the English public schoolboy the chance to travel the world yet always feel at home – not so surprising when you consider that more than half the world was then part of the British Empire. And almost as much as he loved the idea of Empire, the English public schoolboy loved fieldsports – or bloodsports as they are sometimes known today.

At home he might have shot pheasants, rabbits or an occasional deer. In India, Africa and beyond he could shoot – if he was brave enough – anything from alligator to elephant and he was able to do it at a time when the idea of conservation, that there was something wrong with killing wild animals for sport, would have seemed as bizarre as the idea of landing on the moon.

One man who shot his way round the Empire was William Cotton Oswell. While pigsticking in India he'd been gored by a particularly large tusker; in Africa, he once went for days without a bite to eat so intent was he on tracking down a particular elephant; and in the Himalayas he'd bagged some of the world's rarest pheasants.

But after a long day's bird shooting in the wilds of what is now Tanganyika one day in 1887, he and a companion witnessed an encounter that put their most daring days in the shade.

Evening was coming on as they reached the little village of Mabotse where they had been staying. Oswell and his friend stopped at the edge of the village to watch a group of women working in the fields. He noticed a young man standing on the edge of the clearing where the women were working. The young man appeared to be busily flirting with them.

At this point it's worth remembering that, in the 1880s, much of Africa was still unexplored, at least by Europeans, and modern weapons had yet to decimate Africa's population of large mammals.

So it might not have seemed quite so extraordinary when, as Oswell and his companion stood on the edge of that clearing, a lioness rushed out from the deep bush at the edge of the clearing and knocked the young man to the ground where it pinned him while growling fiercely at the women nearby.

Then slowly the lion began to drag the young man away. The women showed no sign of panic by all accounts. There was no screaming. Then, quite calmly, breaking away from the others, a young woman trotted quietly after the lion and, to Oswell's never-ceasing astonishment, she grabbed it by the tail with both hands, dug her heels into the sand and simply hung on. The lion had to slow down.

Hampered by the man in its mouth and the woman dragging behind it, the lion stopped. Immediately the woman let go of the tail, ran a few steps forward and jumped on the lion's back, straddling it like a horse. Oswell, though armed with his rifle and plenty of shot, was so astonished that he didn't have time to react. He simply watched as the woman, gripping the lion between her thighs, proceeded to beat it back and forth across the head and shoulders with her short, heavy-handed hoe.

The woman continued to thrash the lion about the head for several minutes. It then decided it had had enough, dropped the young man and slunk away into the thick undergrowth.

It turned out that the young man was the woman's husband and Oswell, having run over to the couple, discovered that he was none the worse for his ordeal. In fact, he just brushed himself down and began talking quite calmly to his rescuer. The two then wandered off back towards the centre of the village.

Oswell must surely have felt that a man with a rifle was nothing to a woman with a hoe.

THE MAN-EATER OF MANIPUR

INDIA, 1888

Man-eating tigers are almost legendary. Tales of the Raj in those long forgotten, but once hugely popular, books about life in India during British rule, almost invariably include stories of tigers that had decided, for one reason or another, that hunting humans was easier than hunting other game.

There was one particularly savage man-eater on the Manipur border of India and Burma in the early 1880s about which several authors wrote. He escaped capture in forests still relatively unexplored by the logging companies that have now all but destroyed the once vast regions of dense jungle.

Between attacks on humans this particular tiger had grown huge on the villagers' cattle. Stakeouts using large chunks of fresh meat on selected paths that the tiger was known to frequent had proved fruitless and he was only ever seen when he wanted to be seen. Once a local chief inspector of police was out patrolling on his elephant when he saw a massive tiger step out of the bush not sixty feet away and stare at him without any sign of fear.

Unlike almost every other man-eater, the Manipur tiger seemed to know when meat appeared suspicious and he avoided it carefully and presumably regardless of how hungry he was.

On one occasion his audacity got him into the record books. Tigers had often attacked hunters and villagers but they were usually careful to avoid groups of men, knowing that they were likely to be beaten off or shot at. But the man-eater of Tammu, as this tiger was known, once pursued a party of four hunters down a tributary of the Chindwin River.

The men had set off for a day's shooting, little suspecting that they would quickly go from being the pursuers to the pursued.

They had gone a few miles downstream in their canoe – in other words moving with the current – so they were travelling at speed, when one of the men spotted a tiger moving quickly through the dense jungle on the side of the river nearest the boat. He shouted to his friends, but thinking only that this was an unusual sight in daylight.

When the other shooters had one after another agreed that they had seen the animal they noticed that this chance sighting was not accidental. The tiger was not simply moving through the jungle towards some unknown goal. It was galloping steadily along the bank in order to keep pace with their boat. A few moments later, after the men had discussed whether or not they might be mistaken, they saw the tiger take to the water and swim rapidly towards them.

They began to add their greatest rowing efforts to the boat's natural momentum in the current and it was only this that eventually persuaded the tiger to give up as it began to lose ground, but it had reached to within a few yards of the back of the boat before it changed its mind and headed for the bank on the opposite side from which it had launched its attack.

Having reached the other bank the tiger resumed its steady run, keeping pace the whole time with the boat. The men were so astonished that they never thought to load and fire at the animal, but they realised after the tiger had given up the chase and they had time to think that if it had run ahead of the boat and then taken to the water it would have easily reached them.

From some distinctive marks on its head which they later described to an official at their village it was discovered that the men had been chased by the man-eater of Tammu, the tiger that had carried off several children and dozens of cattle. It was never caught or shot despite continuing its depredations for a number of years, but then one year it ceased to appear and it was never seen or heard of again.

THE MOUNTAIN MAN

FRANCE, 1888

Victor Jaccod was a mountain man who spent his life in the French Alps in pursuit of chamois, that delicate elusive deer that is now, quite rightly, protected. But when Victor took wealthy hunters out in pursuit of one of the world's shyest deer he knew that, without him and his lifetime of experience, they would not even see a chamois let alone get the chance to shoot one.

Jaccod's exploits were legendary – one Englishman out shooting with him reported that as they sat and ate lunch together in some high mountain pass Jaccod complained that one of his teeth was hurting. Before the Englishman could express his sympathies Jaccod pulled out his hunting knife and began sawing away at his gums. He'd put his sandwich down while this was going on, which was just as well as the blood poured down his face and on to the snow. The sawing continued until, seemingly satisfied, Jaccod reached up with his free hand and removed a tooth. He held it up to his companion who, once he'd recovered from the shock, said, 'It actually seems to be quite a healthy tooth.' Jaccod is said to have replied, 'Yes, but it was leaning on the tooth next to it and annoying me.'

Jaccod seems to have been an almost fearless gillie as well as being impervious to pain. During a very bad winter in 1888 he sat with his shooting companion on a high snowy ridge enjoying lunch. Tired and knowing that Jaccod could walk through the mountains for another week without rest, the gentleman gunner asked Jaccod to take a cup over to some massive icicles that were hanging nearby and hold the cup under one until it had filled sufficiently to provide enough to drink. Despite the deep snow and blizzards that had blown for days it was a rare sunny afternoon and the surface of the snow had become slippery. As Jaccod moved towards the icicles his heels suddenly shot up and he plunged fifteen feet into a steep crevasse, which had remained in the shade and was hard ice. When he hit this hard ice he began to slide faster down its steep slope towards a rock face that dropped sheer to the valley five hundred feet below. The shooter watched helplessly, convinced that Jaccod was as good as dead, but the wily mountain man kept his head and, by keeping himself feet foremost, and digging with his iron-spiked heels into the frozen surface, he managed to stop his slide just two feet short of the massive drop.

He had travelled more than sixty yards and the iron spikes on his boots were bent completely flat. The sportsman climbed round the crevasse to meet Jaccod, expecting to find him badly shaken and glad of assistance. Instead he came up out of the crevasse with a broad smile and only commented that he'd enjoyed his slide.

Jaccod's exploits continued when he spotted a poacher on the shoot that he was paid to guard. The poacher was armed with a rifle and Jaccod, similarly armed, set off in pursuit. The poacher having got some way ahead of Jaccod dropped into a hollow and prepared his ambush. When Jaccod appeared he felt a bullet whistle past his face and instinctively fired back – normally, and despite his brilliant tracking skills and knowledge of the mountains, Jaccod could not hit a haystack, but this time he fired from the hip and the bullet sped true and killed the poacher outright.

Jaccod went straight into the town and gave himself up. He found the local policeman then the magistrate; neither, despite his pleas, would arrest him. In the end he got the keys from the local sheriff and locked himself up in the town gaol. In due course he was tried and acquitted on the grounds of self-defence.

He was, however, fined as his shooting permit had expired two days before the incident with the poacher. He had tried to renew the permit but had been unable to find the appropriate official, but the authorities felt this was an insufficient excuse.

THE SHOOTER WHO HATED SHOOTING

IRELAND, 1888

Deafness and headaches are a constant problem for the shooting man, but it is only in recent years that the full extent of the damage caused by repeated gunshot to the hearing has been fully understood. Now many guns wear ear defenders both for clay shooting and game shooting, although older more conservative guns see this, bizarrely, as something rather effeminate.

In late Victorian and early Edwardian days when organised shooting in Britain reached a peak that it is never likely to reach again, the most enthusiastic guns – men like Lord de Grey and Ralph Payne Gallwey – would quite regularly fire their guns as many as 1,500 times in a day. The result was increasing deafness and the emergence of the stereotype of the elderly gun as red-faced (too much drink) overweight (too much good food) and deaf as a post.

Many guns denied that shooting so much had any effect at all, but others suffered horribly. There is a story that Sir Edward Guinness, while shooting at an estate in Ireland, bribed the keeper to ensure that, all day, he would draw pegs that ensured he was as far as possible from any of the shooting. His head hurt so badly after just a few shots that he was far happier just to be out with the other guns. As a result he spent the rest of the day standing doing nothing in the middle of various fields. Having to shoot would have ruined his day by giving him a phenomenal headache. Instead he just had to put up with mumbled complaints from the keeper about 'that mad gentleman over there'.

TRIAL BY FIRE

PERTHSHIRE, 1888

Two gillies employed on the Duke of Atholl's estate in Perthshire spotted a poacher – who also happened to be the local blacksmith – and chased him for several miles across the moor. Eventually they caught up with him. 'I'm only having a little fun – it's just for my own diversion I'm out on the hill,' he said.

'Well, we must take you anyway,' said the two gillies who'd seen the blacksmith quite clearly shoot one of the duke's deer.

The blacksmith was taken down to Glen Tilt and brought before the duke. The duke gave the poacher a choice – he could either go to Perth Gaol for three months or stand a shot from the duke's rifle at 100 paces. The blacksmith said he would stand the shot. The ground was measured out by one of the duke's servants and the blacksmith took up his position.

'Place him with his front right side towards me and give me my best rifle,' said the duke.

The duke raised his rifle and took aim while all around the hill men and gillies and estate servants watched with open mouths. The duke aimed long and steady, but the blacksmith never flinched – eventually the duke fired and only the rifle cap exploded.

'Give me another rifle,' roared the duke, 'and make sure it is better loaded.' The second rifle misfired too – as it was bound to do since the duke had arranged the whole thing himself.

'The gods have blessed you today,' said the duke and then he told his servants to give the blacksmith as much whisky as he liked.

'But mark me,' said the duke to the blacksmith, 'you are a brave man but if you come after my deer ever again my gun will not again misfire.'

The blacksmith agreed to steer clear of the duke's deer in future.

HUGE BAGS

NORFOLK, 1889

Thomas, the 6th Lord Walsingham, is generally considered one of the greatest shots who ever lived. Only Lord de Grey was said to surpass him in skill, although to the modern eye both men would have had little excuse for not being brilliant shots given the extraordinary amount of shooting they did. Of course, part of the reason for this is that from about 1890 until the outbreak of the Great War in 1914 shooting became a massive industry with the emphasis more and more on huge numbers of birds being driven over the guns. After the war such excess, even among the upper class from whom excess had always been expected, had become unacceptable.

But even by the standards of Edwardian excess Lord Walsingham's shooting record is extraordinary. On one day he killed 1,070 grouse – a rate later calculated at $2^1/_3$ birds a minute. To do it he fired 1,510 cartridges during twenty drives and twice killed three birds in the air with just one shot. Of course he needed some serious backup to do it – he used three guns, which were continually reloaded, by his two loaders and his cartridge boy. Walsingham swung the guns and pulled the trigger, but to anyone watching the whole thing must have been a blur.

Walsingham was an intriguing man. He studied insects with a passion and, like so many Victorians, amassed a huge collection of birds' eggs and stuffed birds that he'd shot himself. When the Natural History Museum in London started its collection of hummingbirds it was Walsingham who went out to South America and shot them all – he used tiny dust shot to ensure that the birds were damaged as little as possible. We may gasp now at the horror of doing such a thing, but it is perhaps unfair to judge the standards of one age by those of another. At the time Walsingham was doing science a favour.

Walsingham's strangest day's shooting came in January 1889 when in one day he shot the biggest and most varied bag ever recorded: it included thirty-nine pheasants, six partridges, twenty-three mallard duck, six gadwall duck, four pochard duck, one goldeneye, seven teal, three swans, a woodcock, three snipe, a woodpigeon, two herons, sixty-five coots, two moorhens, nine hares, sixteen rabbits, an otter, a pike (which was shot as it swam through shallow water) and a big rat.

Walsingham's love of shooting was such that he neglected his estates, made some appalling investment decisions and eventually became bankrupt. It didn't help when the notoriously greedy Edward VII took the shooting at Walsingham's estate at Merton and in one season emptied the fabulous wine cellar that had taken generations to build up.

ARMOUR-PLATED CORDUROYS

ESSEX, 1890

Our ancestors' rather blasé attitude to safety and other people's property produced some extraordinary shooting days.

One such day occurred on a shoot at a small farm in Essex, where two or three friends met each weekend for a few hours' sport.

The shoot consisted of about 120 acres, but nicely broken up and with plenty of cover. Game was usually abundant, lots of birds and every bank holding rabbits. The day had been hot, and the friends had been round and round the boundaries, driving the birds in towards the middle of the farm, where there was a beautiful field of mangolds of about seven acres.

The only problem with this field was that it was a very dangerous place to shoot; a lane bounded it on one side, while four or five labourers' cottages were dotted round the border of the field.

But the shooters had put several coveys of birds right into the middle of the field, and they just couldn't resist following them. The route they chose meant there was one cottage right in front of them as they moved off.

Almost directly, up got some birds, one swerving low to the right. Instinctively one of the guns swung after him and fired, bringing him down.

But imagine the gun's horror when a quavering voice came from the cottage garden, 'Hi! You've shot me.'

The man who'd fired the shot went up to the fence and

looked over, expecting to see a mangled mass of humanity. However, out toddled a very old man, with no visible wounds upon him, who proceeded to explain matters. It appeared that he'd been crouching down behind the garden hedge, eagerly looking on, hoping to see some sport when the offending shot was fired. He managed to slew himself around, and just a stray shot or two hit him in the rear, and he was decidedly more frightened than hurt.

After much investigation a shot mark was found on the old man's enormously thick corduroys, which had actually acted as armour plating and flattened the little piece of lead. The three guns made the old boy very happy by presenting him with half a crown, and advising him to stay out of his garden and go upstairs until the shooting was over.

The old man was very penitent and evidently thought he was quite to blame in the matter and trotted off indoors.

The three friends continued to shoot the field and this time a mass of birds got up, scattering all over the place. Bang! bang! went the guns; there was a tinkle of glass. Then came the voice they were dreading.

'Hi! You've shot me again!'

This time they'd sent a charge of shot right through the old man's window, most fortunately missing him, but shattering the glass and frightening the poor old fellow half to death.

He came out again and in appealing accents said: 'Where am I to go? You shoot me in the garden and when I go upstairs you shoot me there too.' They gave the old man another half crown and left the birds in peace; the game was not worth the candle.

BETTING ON THE GUNS

YORKSHIRE, 1890

When the Victorians and Edwardians went shooting they did not have to worry about anti-bloodsports people turning up and spoiling their fun. Nor would the newspapers of the day have published anything suggesting that the aristocracy were lazy, good-for-nothing parasites who lived on the sweat of their tenants and spent their days slaughtering thousands of fat, lazy, virtually domesticated birds. No. Until the Second World War the lower orders were far more deferential than they are now and it was accepted, among the working and middle classes, that the wealthy were a breed apart and above criticism.

This didn't mean that the landed gentry escaped entirely unscathed, however. In the days when transport was still by horse and cart (and railway for those who could afford it) the country people had to find their entertainment locally.

At shoots at Welbeck House in the later part of the nineteenth century and at estates in Yorkshire and Durham where coal mines were within easy reach, it was common to find groups of miners, farm workers, ship builders, navvies and local villagers standing just a few yards behind the guns, for shooting in those days was very much a spectator sport.

Many guns complained that their shooting suffered from the pressure of a hundred pairs of eyes trained on their every move, but if the spectators were on a bit of common land nearby or on a public footpath they just had to put up with it.

At Welbeck on one occasion each gun found hundreds of

132

spectators grouped behind him at every drive. This made shooting difficult enough but it got worse when the spectators, mostly miners, began to shout encouragement and praise if their man happened to be shooting well. Others found that when they missed a bird there was a roar of disapproval and individual shouts of 'You're rubbish!' or worse. *Nothing changed*

At one point during the day the spectators started taking bets on who would shoot what and when and it is said that several miners went home hundreds of pounds better off.

It must be one of the few examples where the upper classes were used by the lower for their entertainment.

FASCINATING GREYLAG

LOCH LEVEN, 1890

You are never so close to nature than when in pursuit of it. That may be a tired old cliché but there is some truth in it and many shooting men would go so far as to say that more than half the pleasure of shooting comes simply from being out and about in the wilder parts of the countryside. Occasionally the naturalist in every shooting man spots something that all the scientists have missed. The Victorian sportsman John Guille Millais is a case in point. His most fascinating observations concerned the greylag geese on Loch Leven.

He'd planned his usual shooting outings on the loch for the winter of 1890, but decided he could shift the odds massively in his favour if he dug a pit, covered it with camouflage and then shot the geese as they flew over. Simply hiding in a depression or behind a wall, which was what he usually did, was effective, but the geese tended to see him and flare at the last minute. The pit would hide him completely. So the pit was duly dug and covered with muddy branches and other scraps to make it indistinguishable from the rest of the foreshore and early one morning Millais settled down to wait. What he saw over the next two hours had never been observed before and, though it had little to do directly with shooting, Millais would not have been in a position to notice it had he not been out with his gun.

First a lone goose came winging in from the distance, but rather than make its way directly overhead the bird carefully quartered the ground as if checking that all was well and no danger lurked. Having given the whole area a careful once-over the goose departed back the way it had come without once alighting.

Fascinated, Millais forgot all about his gun and simply watched through a tiny gap in his camouflage roof. A few moments after the lone goose had departed a small party of half a dozen geese gradually appeared high up on the distant horizon. Like the lone goose they checked over the ground flying this way and that before swinging back round and returning the way they'd come. A few minutes later the sky was filled with geese. The early birds had obviously returned to the main flock and indicated to them that all was apparently well. Without hesitating the huge flock circled once and landed all about Millais who remained carefully concealed in his hide, hardly daring to breathe.

Immediately they landed all the geese began to feed except for six birds evenly distributed around the edge of the rough circle of geese. After ten minutes a feeding goose walked over to one of the sentries and tapped it on the back with its beak. Immediately, the goose that had been on the lookout began feeding and the other goose took over sentry duty. And so it continued as the geese took turn and turn about feeding and watching.

But despite all their precautions the geese had missed the lone gunner. Having got himself in position Millais thought he ought to try a shot so he simply stood up and poked his head out through the top of his pit. He later wrote that the roar of goose wing beats that followed was almost terrifying in its intensity. Indeed so great was the noise that despite firing both barrels Millais went home empty-handed that day.

HILL MEN OF THE HIMALAYAS

NEPAL, 1890

Ibex shooting in the Himalayas was extremely dangerous, not because the ibex themselves would ever fight back – far from it – but because the terrain, with its icy paths and deep, snow-covered ravines was so treacherous. But there were many British hunters for whom the extreme danger was pretty much the main attraction. The Victorian and Edwardian eras produced an attitude in the men sent out to serve the Empire that courted danger and scorned hardship however great. It was exactly the sort of attitude that enabled so many young men to march stick in hand towards heavy German machine guns in the Great War.

The ibex is basically a goat, but a very beautiful one with magnificent curved horns, and it was these curved horns that the British sportsman coveted.

Major Neville Taylor was perhaps the most fanatical ibex hunter who ever lived. He spent years during the 1880s and 1890s traversing the most dangerous parts of the Himalayas in search of the highly secretive and elusive ibex. He bagged many fine animals but also saw killed numerous trackers and Sherpas who accompanied his various expeditions.

Once, having missed a relatively easy shot at a particularly fine animal – a miss that reduced him to tears – Taylor was lucky enough to have a chance at another ibex just an hour or so later. Determined not to miss again he took careful aim, fired and was astonished to see the ibex bound down a snowy slope. He fired again at the running animal and saw the bullet splash into the snow next to him. Two more animals crossed his sights and each time he fired he seemed to miss. It was one of the worst days he'd ever had on the mountains, but then Lassoo, a local tribesman who accompanied Taylor for years said that in fact the major had hit an ibex. Taylor, already extremely experienced, was astonished at this and insisted that he'd missed every time. But the local man knew best and spying further down the wide expanse of snow he saw the fallen ibex. But unfortunately it was slipping along the icy surface of the snow and with every second it gathered speed until it pitched over the edge of a ravine and disappeared from sight.

'Damn,' said the major, 'his horns will be smashed to bits.' Despite the assumption that it was pointless, the major and his Sherpas set off for the edge of the ravine to see if it was possible to retrieve the ibex. They crawled carefully through the snow down the steep slope to the edge of the cliff, knowing that if they lost their grip they would slide over the edge in an instant.

The ibex had fallen about halfway down the ravine – about 200 feet – and had become wedged on a rocky outcrop with its head hanging over the edge and the horns undamaged. But how on earth were they to retrieve them?

It was at this point that Major Taylor saw something that stayed in his memory for the rest of his life. He was himself a very brave man, but what he saw that day made him realise that he could never compete with the bravery of the hill men of the Himalayas. Despite the sub-zero temperatures two of the Sherpas took off their coats and their rope shoes and socks and climbed down the sheer rock face – littered with patches of deadly ice – until they had reached the rocky outcrop where the ibex lay. The major said later that he simply could not believe his eyes. At various stages of the climb the two men seemed to perch on one toe for minutes at a time while a hand searched out a tiny firm hold.

'I would not have gone with them for all the gold of the

Indies,' the major said. 'It was only what I saw this day that made me realise what a hill man can do and that no European could ever hope to attain their skill in the most inhospitable conditions.'

Once they'd reached the animal the hill men had a further difficulty. As it was dead they could not eat it despite the fact that the party had not eaten properly for days. The problem was the strict Muslim rule that the animal had to be killed while it still had a breath in its body. As they had taken some time to get to the ibex they could not 'get a breath' out of it as they said. But the horns were removed and by what seemed like another miracle the two Sherpas were able to climb back up the icy rock face to safety.

IMPERSONATING A TOFF

ENGLAND, 1890

Published in 1890, an anonymous poacher's memoirs caused a minor sensation in Victorian England. The book was denounced by the clergy who, then as now, denounced pretty much anything of interest, and questions were asked in the House of Commons. One or two M.P.s thought the publishers ought to be prosecuted. But whatever the rights and wrongs of the case, the book is filled with fascinating memories of rural England in the middle decades of the nineteenth century. Most of the poacher's stories have to do with the extraordinary obsession of the aristocracy with game preservation. One can understand the need to preserve pheasants, for example, from poachers – even perhaps poachers with starving families – but in the 1840s and 50s, it was still a serious offence to catch another man's rabbit even if that rabbit had strayed into your garden. And this at a time when rabbit numbers were approaching plague proportions.

But our anonymous poacher was too crafty for the authorities and in a lifetime devoted to poaching he was never caught – and when one reads his book it is easy to see why, for he was remarkably clever, ingenious and well read. A sort of gentleman poacher, to use the jargon of the time.

The anonymous poacher's finest hour came when he impersonated what he described as a 'toff'. He planned the raid with great care, though he never says how he obtained the right kind of clothing. But on the day in question he dressed in

139

his finest suit and persuaded an accomplice to dress in servant's clothes and carry his bag. The two men went on to an estate which they knew had recently changed owners. The poacher told his accomplice to make sure he doffed his cap as often as possible and adopted a suitably servile air. Once into the field the poacher began to shoot the game that was everywhere. The estate was criminally overstocked with birds and within an hour the poacher had shot more than thirty.

Then out of the corner of his eye he spotted the keeper. When the keeper spotted the poacher's suit of clothes he assumed he was a gentleman and doffed his hat. The poacher, in his best clipped tones, immediately treated the keeper as if he were the lowest of the low and the keeper was even more convinced that this was someone important. The poacher congratulated the keeper on the quality of his birds and said he would mention this to his master (i.e. the keeper's master) who was a great friend. In the 1840s no servant would dare to question a social superior and so the keeper simply helped as much as he could, even to the extent of setting off to collect a handcart to carry the poacher's birds. As soon as the keeper was out of sight the poacher and his accomplice ran into a nearby wood and brought out a donkey. The game was piled high into the panniers on its back and the two disappeared, never to be seen again.

JACKAL SNAPPER

INDIA, 1890

A British ship was riding at anchor in the Hooghli River some miles downstream from Calcutta. One of the ship's young officers decided he would go jackal shooting along the banks of one of the tributaries of the sacred river Ganges, a place where it was known that these wild dogs came down to eat and drink. Mostly what they ate were the bodies of the drowned, which tended to come ashore in one particular place, and it was to this place that the young officer went early one morning in 1890.

The young officer had shot several wild dogs when he came across a very young jackal puppy. He didn't have the heart to shoot it so he looked around for some way to take it back to the ship with him. Nothing could be found so he took off his belt and tied it round the young jackal's neck. At that very instant the young officer was struck by the tail of a huge alligator that had virtually thrown itself up the gravel bank. The young sailor fell on his face in about eighteen inches of water, but in the very act of falling he swung the puppy, which was still at the end of his belt, into the river. The poor animal was instantly snapped up by the alligator and devoured wholesale – even the belt and buckle vanished into its maw.

The sailor admitted later that he was extremely lucky that the puppy had taken the edge off the alligator's appetite long enough for him to drag himself out of the water and away from danger.

MAD DOGS AND ENGLISHMEN

INDIA, 1890

Colonel Fred Markham was a fanatical shot who seemed to be particularly interested in trying to rear or at least tame the offspring of animals he'd shot. Once in India he shot a wild dog and then did his utmost to keep its two pups alive. One died quickly but the other survived and became devoted to the colonel, but when he tried to train it as a gundog things went badly wrong. On their first day out the dog was behaving wonderfully well, following its master attentively and at heel, but then they passed a flock of sheep and in an instant the little wild dog, no bigger than a Yorkshire terrier, was gone, belting across the field in pursuit of them. It grabbed the biggest sheep by the underside of its belly and hung on for half a mile across the field before the colonel could catch up with it and drag it off.

The little wild dog would allow itself to be petted unless it was feeding, at which time no one could go anywhere near it. On the day of its first shoot – which also proved to be its last – the little wild dog ate every pheasant shot by its master even though during training sessions using dead pheasants it had brought each one back to its master's hand with no damage at all.

Nothing daunted, the colonel kept the little dog as a pet until it contracted distemper and died, but refusing to be beaten he then tried to train a little orphan wild boar, with equally disastrous results.

POACHER'S TRICKS

SURREY, 1890

A keen young shooting man was best friend with the local poacher who often took him up on to the common land near Guildford – this was in the 1890s when this was still a remote rural area – where the shooting was free, although as a result of course there was very little to shoot. The young man had an occasional try for a rabbit, but rarely even saw a pheasant.

But one day the poacher decided they'd take their guns and shoot the edge of the local landowner's ground, which was alive with pheasants. They bagged a couple of pheasants but then the noise of their shooting brought out the keeper and they had to make a run for it.

Next time out the old poacher said they should both take their guns, but they'd also take a silent weapon from the poacher's armoury. The young man called in at the poacher's isolated little cottage on the appointed day. While their morning tea was brewing the poacher took a few pages from a newspaper and cut them into eight-inch squares. He then twisted the squares into little cone-shaped packets and fitted them together one inside the other and popped them inside a sack.

'What on earth are they for?' asked the young man.

'You bide and see,' said the old poacher, who next gathered together a bag of barley grains. Finally, he gathered together two more items – a thick, sharp-pointed iron poker about two feet long and a small bottle with a wooden screw top and a brush going down through the top into whatever liquid lay within.

The bottle, the young man discovered later, contained birdlime – a sort of sticky glue. The two men then set off across the fields, the poacher with his bag of bits and pieces, the young man, still hopeful of a shot or two, with his gun in hand. They walked about three miles until they came to a little-used road. They went along this for some distance until they came to a gate. Here the poacher stopped and told the young man to wait and keep an eye out in case anyone should come along the road.

On the other side of the gate was a field about two hundred yards across and on its far side there was a wood. The poacher set off across the field disturbing a few pheasants as he went, some of which ran while others flew into the wood. When he was within twenty yards of the trees he stopped and pulled out his iron poker. He pushed it into the ground and worked it to make a hole a good bit greater in diameter that the poker itself. Having made his hole he took out one of the paper cones and popped it into the hole. He then tipped in a few grains of barley and finally painted the edge of the inside of the cup with his birdlime brush. He then moved three or four yards away and repeated the whole operation. Continuing in this way, but keeping always parallel with the edge of the wood he made and filled about nine holes.

Pheasants will always run away from a stranger but, if they see him lingering near their home wood, especially if he stoops much of the time, will keep their eyes fixed on him and the minute he goes they will come out to investigate what he's been up to. Before the poacher had got back to the gate where his young friend waited, more than a dozen pheasants had come out to see what was going on.

The young man was astonished to see what happened next. A cock pheasant ran quickly across the grass and dipped its head into one of the holes to get at the barley. A second later, when it withdrew its head, it was covered with the paper bag which the birdlime had stuck fast. The pheasant began to shake its head vigorously, but the paper bag stayed firmly in place. He then tried scratching at his head with his foot. Still no good. In the space of a minute three more birds were hopping around with paper bags on their heads. The young man offered to go and get them in case their strange appearance and behaviour might act as a warning to others, but the poacher knew better and the two simply waited. Within ten minutes nine pheasants were bagged. It was at this point that the old poacher pulled out a thin canvas bag and walked quickly out to where the birds were staggering around. Within seconds they had allowed themselves to be picked up as quietly as possible.

When they returned to the poacher's cottage he told the young man that they could get a better price for the birds if they sold them to a man who would keep them for his aviary.

And that was the end of a successful day's shooting when not a shot was fired.

STOATS AT PLAY

ENGLAND, 1890

It's often been said that the best thing about shooting is not the shooting itself but the things you come across when you are out shooting. And some of the most extraordinary observations in natural history have certainly been made by people wandering the fields with gun in hand and dog at heel.

The zoologist C.B. Moffat was out shooting one evening towards the end of 1890 when he came across a group of three stoats playing on the open road – an unusual enough event in itself for stoats are shy animals and rarely stray far from cover. The stoats had a hole at the side of the road under the fence to which they momentarily returned as Moffat drew near. He stood perfectly still and a few minutes later they came out of their hole and resumed their game.

The animals seemed to be young, but Moffat knew enough about animals in general to know that they were actually fully grown, which made their play even more extraordinary. As they dashed about the three animals continually called out a strange 'curoo, curoo, curoo' sound, a sound which increased in intensity the faster they ran. For the most part their game consisted of dashing back and forth and crisscrossing over and under each other each time they met in the middle of the road. Many times they leaped in the air as they reached each other or deliberately jumped at the same time and crashed into each other and all apparently just for the fun of it.

Then the stoats began to go through a most peculiar ritual.

Individually, or two at a time, or even all three together, they pressed their noses to the ground, emitted a little shriek and then ran another foot or so before repeating the process. Then they began to play with each other like kittens, each knocking his fellows down, but gently and then running a little and waiting, it almost seemed, to be themselves knocked down by their fellows. One of the three then began to turn very graceful somersaults exactly as a small boy might do it. First he placed his head very deliberately on the ground, then turned gracefully over and righted himself just in time to avoid falling on his back, by standing erect on his hind legs. The same stoat did this again and again but the other two animals never attempted it.

After some time, one of the three ran up a tree and waited, leaving the other two on the ground. These two remaining then began to play a game with Moffat, who later said it was the most barefaced piece of impudence he'd ever experienced either from man or beast.

The stoats knew perfectly well they were dealing with a man not a tree or fence post for their sense of smell is extremely well developed and for most animals the scent of man is more terrifying than the scent of lion or tiger.

The stoats' game consisted in each trying to outdo the other in daring how close they would come to him before darting away shrieking with what almost seemed like laughter. The two came towards him with a graceful and almost joyous trot, side by side and cooing the whole time. Then suddenly both would turn tail and bolt, almost falling over in their haste to get away and convinced that this man was after them. When Moffat didn't move they again bounded along towards him with the same agile grace and sociable expression. Once again when they were within two or three feet of Moffat they turned and ran, emitting signals of alarm that seemed almost mocking. After a while one of the two remaining stoats took up a grandstand seat on a nearby post and watched the last of the three continue the game.

The last stoat continued the game, each time getting closer to Moffat's legs until he was as close as six inches. Moffat was convinced he would run up his trouser legs but on his final pass when he was almost upon him the stoat on the post issued a warning whistle and he bounded towards him instead. Then he went back to Moffat and sat behind him six inches from his feet. Knowing the stoat's swift tree-climbing abilities Moffat became uneasy, but the stoat was soon circling him once again and cooing at every turn. Finally he walked over to Moffat's stick on which his hand rested, climbed up it with his forefeet and began licking contentedly. The instant Moffat moved the three stoats vanished and despite visiting the place on his rambles on future days he never saw them again. Half a day's shooting had been wasted, but it was an experience Moffat would not have missed for the world.

THE WHITE QUEEN

SCOTLAND, 1890

Charles McInnes spent four winters, starting in 1890, in pursuit of a greylag goose that returned each year to the Tay estuary. This was no ordinary greylag – McInnes called it the White Queen – and he was so determined to shoot it that for those four seasons he neglected his job and his family. Morning and evening he was out on the estuary waiting and hoping against hope for a shot. He hardly bothered with the other geese and almost drowned on several occasions so desperate were his attempts to get within range. He often saw the White Queen, but somehow she was always a little too far away or he was in the wrong place at the wrong time.

Then, towards the end of the fourth winter after he'd first seen her, McInnes saw the White Queen coming steadily towards the ditch in which he'd been hiding. He could hardly believe his luck, but as she approached she began to flare away and there was a chance that she would pass over just out of range. McInnes couldn't bear to lose her again so he fired and far away she tumbled out of the sky.

Unfortunately for McInnes she fell in the sea and into a racing tide. He threw his gun and bag to the ground and began to run along the mudflats desperately trying to keep pace with her, then he plunged into the freezing sea, wading through the water until he became stuck fast in the mud up to his waist. He watched helplessly as the bird drifted further away.

McInnes was a big, strong man and after a few frightening

moments he managed to pull himself out of the mud – minus his boots – and back on firmer ground he dashed along the mud following the direction of the goose. Having got parallel with it again he stripped off completely, dived in and began swimming out to sea – and this in temperatures well below freezing.

A few hundred yards out he hit a sandbank and realised that despite the fact that he was now in sight of the goose he couldn't get over the sandbank. He watched as the bird drifted towards him but on the other side of the bank. At one point it was just ten feet away, but after four years of waiting he had to watch as the White Queen sailed majestically past him and then began to drift out to sea. Exhausted by now, McInnes was just able to get back to shore where he collapsed hardly able to move or breathe. He lay on the sand shivering and unable to get up. At last he made a supreme effort and staggered, still completely naked, to a farmhouse some two miles away. He vowed never again to go shooting without a dog.

POINT-BLANK RANGE

AFRICA, 1891

William Cotton Oswell, though now forgotten, was one of the great popular heroes of Victorian England. Strong, brave, good-looking and obsessed with adventure he travelled extensively in Africa at a time when much of that continent had still to be explored by Europeans. He was a great friend of David Livingstone who freely admitted that without Oswell's knowledge of the interior he, Livingstone, would never have completed his famous journeys.

On one occasion Livingstone sent him sixteen oxen as a present 'for your invaluable help with the natives'.

Throughout more than thirty years in southern Africa Oswell used the same 10 bore muzzle-loading Purdey rifle. He claimed it never let him down despite its appalling appearance. Battered by endless encounters with rocks and trees, rhino and elephant it looked more like a rusty iron pipe than a rifle – one friend said he would not have used it to prop up his beans.

Oswell's shooting technique was singularly dangerous. He didn't stalk his game, which was the technique adopted by most Victorian big-game hunters. Instead he would spot a herd or an individual animal through his binoculars and then, either alone or with one companion, he would kick his pony on and chase the rhino or elephant until it was within range. He'd then leap off the pony's back, crouch and fire. He insisted that for rhino and buffalo it was absolutely essential to shoot from a crouching position; what he didn't say was that he liked to be within fifteen paces of the animal when he fired.

Rhino and elephant often charged him as he leaped from his horse, but there is no record of his ever making a run for it. Instead he would crouch and fire and despite the sorry state of his old rifle it never jammed or misfired. If it had he would certainly have been killed. Oswell claimed that the reason he hardly ever wounded an animal was precisely because he made sure he shot them at point-blank range. Very few other big-game hunters adopted this point-blank technique and those who were foolhardy enough to try it did not usually survive long. It was probably Oswell's absolute confidence in his abilities that saved him. 'If you are afraid of dying, don't try it,' he once observed. 'It will make you nervous and you'll miss or, worse, you'll wound your quarry.'

Oswell would spend twelve hours a day in the saddle, seven days a week for months at a time. He described seeing springbok herds so vast that it took half a day for them to pass. Sometimes if they were shot at they would simply stand their ground while a single edible blade of grass could be found and regardless of how many of their number lay dead around them.

But Oswell's most extraordinary day's shooting in a lifetime of extraordinary experiences came as he hunted a single huge buffalo. Oswell always reckoned that the most dangerous animal in Africa was not the rhino, the elephant or even the lion – it was the buffalo. Slow to anger, the buffalo, when roused, would fight to the death and with its blood up it was a very difficult animal to kill. Hunters had reported hitting buffalo a dozen times in apparently fatal spots only to see the animal shake its head and charge again.

On the day in question Oswell, riding his favourite pony, had followed the fleeing buffalo for miles until it began to tire. He then did something he regretted for the rest of his life. Despite his insistence that the only safe shot at a buffalo was from a crouching position on the ground he took a chance and fired at the buffalo from the back of the pony. No sooner had he fired than the buffalo dropped. Stone dead. Oswell was delighted with himself and, having seen the buffalo go down, he began to slow his pony as he rode up to and a little past the fallen animal. No sooner had he passed the dead animal than he heard a strange noise and glancing back he saw the buffalo leap to its feet and begin its charge. Oswell dug in his spurs in a vain attempt to get ahead of the charging animal, but it was no good. In an instant the buffalo had its horns under the belly of the horse, and horse and man were thrown into the air. Oswell was knocked unconscious by the fall and when he woke an hour later he found his horse nearby with its stomach torn out. There was no trace of the buffalo and no sign of its blood. For the rest of his life Oswell believed that the buffalo had tricked him, but he never again shot a large animal from horseback.

One curious thing about Oswell is that he is pretty much the only Victorian big game hunter who expressed regret about the numbers of animals he had killed. He felt he could only justify himself on the grounds that the dozens, sometimes hundreds of Africans who accompanied him, always ate the meat from every animal he shot. 'These were hungry people,' he once said, 'and at least I helped feed them.'

TWO IN THE AIR

DEVON, 1891

Among the most bizarre and eccentric clubs in Britain has to be the Woodcock Club. To join you must have shot two woodcock in the air (or nearly in the air) at the same time. One has to be shot with the cartridge from one barrel; the other must then fall to the second barrel. It's a very difficult trick to perform, not just because woodcock tend to be solitary birds, but also because there aren't that many about and when they get up they fly very erratically and are easy to miss.

One day in 1891 the keeper on a Devon estate took his master's son and a friend rough shooting through the local woods, which in those far off halcyon days were rarely shot and consequently full of game of all sorts.

As they walked along a narrow ride a rabbit crossed to the right and one of the young men took a pot shot at it. The instant he fired – and missed – another rabbit crossed to the left and without thinking the young man took a snap shot at it as it disappeared across a narrow track into the thick undergrowth.

The keeper and the two young men searched in vain for either rabbit, but to their utter astonishment they found two woodcock about three yards apart but in the exact line along which the young man had fired.

CONTINENTAL GILLIE

CORSICA, 1892

Continental shooting men and their gillies could be just as eccentric as their British cousins. A professional hunter in Corsica – professional hunter being the equivalent of the Scottish gillie – known as Le Jeune had been wanted by the police for years because he could not resist doing something if he knew it was illegal.

It was always small things, but put together they amounted to a career in crime that the police could not ignore. As a result he lived permanently in the mountains. If he wanted a fire he would light a whole pine tree – itself illegal – and he seemed entirely fearless except when necessity or desire drove him into Calacuccia where the police were based. He told the English hunters who employed him that he had been on the run for two years and if he could avoid capture for a further three the statute of limitations would relieve him of further fears. No one knew what his first offence had been but it must have been more serious than burning trees.

But with the curious laws in force in a country where religion was and probably still is taken very seriously, it transpired that Le Jeune could not be arrested in certain public places on feast days nor on any Sundays. English tourists began to suspect that the police did not much want to arrest him anyway on the grounds that it was cheaper to leave him at liberty than to lock him up.

Once a group of Englishmen hired Le Jeune to take them

hunting. The night before they were due to enjoy their first day stalking deer, a friend of Le Jeune's, the local priest, visited him as he sat drinking with the party of Englishmen. Despite all attempts to put him off the priest insisted on joining them the following day. When they met in the morning the priest still wore his cassock but had slung a big bandolier over it.

By lunchtime on the following day the Englishmen had seen nothing and were beginning to think they were wasting their time. But then things began to liven up. As they stood around a fire Le Jeune set himself alight, but with a big burnt patch on his coat he seemed not in the least concerned. Le Jeune then set off on a detour below a ridge along which the others decided to wait. They waited for hours but Le Jeune disappeared completely until evening when he joined the rest of the party at a remote cabin. The Englishmen were paying him and were understandably cross, but Le Jeune just smiled and went straight to bed.

Next morning shortly after the party set off Le Jeune disappeared again. This time the rest of the party split into search parties to look for him. He was found eventually and again there was no explanation for his absence.

At the end of their shooting holiday the Englishmen decided that the sport had been terrible because both Le Jeune and the priest saw shooting as an excuse to wander about the mountains with guests who invariably had plenty of money and bought wine and good food, but Le Jeune at least gave one of the Englishmen a parting gift. He made a great show of presenting his tobacco pouch. When the Englishman demurred, saying he thought the old man (he was old despite his name) might find it difficult to replace, Le Jeune brushed that objection aside saying that he had only to catch, kill and skin another cat.

The pouch was merely the skin of that animal's trunk sewn up at one of the two open ends.

DRINKS FOR THE BEATERS

ANTRIM, 1892

A shooting man's best friend is his hip flask. Shooting men hate to see such a thing in print because they like to present an image of sober seriousness to the rest of the public, but no shoot would be complete without a wee dram, particularly on a cold winter's morning.

Keepers and gillies are traditionally fond of a drink but this would rarely develop into alcoholism, probably because a drunken keeper would soon be an unemployed keeper. Similar constraints, for obvious reasons, have not applied to members of the landowning aristocracy.

Lord Massereene and Ferrard, who owned an estate in County Antrim, found that as he grew older his enthusiasm for sport declined as his fondness for alcohol increased. He was apparently quite a decent employer by the standards of the time and his keepers and beaters must have enjoyed the shoot rituals he established. One such ritual was enormously popular and it meant that his Lordship was never short of staff.

Shoot days always began in the same way. Massereene would get a household servant to bring out a table and a chair. These would be placed on the lawn in front of the house. Massereene would sit at the table with a row of bottles in front of him containing brandy, rum, gin and whisky. He would then line his beaters up in front of him. Each beater was given a number rather than a letter, which was the practice on most estates at the time.

In crisp autocratic tones Massereene would then begin.

'Number one. Now, what'll you have?'

'I'll be quite happy with whatever your Lordship chooses,' number one – well versed in the routine – would reply.

'Well now,' came his Lordship's reply, 'I should have said that brandy's the fellow for you.'

He would then take the brandy bottle, pour a glass and drink it himself.

'Oh yes, definitely. That's your brandy,' he would say before selecting another glass, filling it and handing it to the bemused beater.

This ritual would be repeated until all the beaters had been offered whatever drink Massereene thought most suitable, and of course for each drink he handed out, his Lordship had one himself.

There seemed to be no logic to his Lordship's decision to award any one beater a particular drink. He just chose at random and then reached for the appropriate bottle.

Legend has it that Massereene, who was not a particularly keen shot, much preferred this early morning ritual to hanging about with a gun waiting for a few pheasants to fly over. It was also said that, on particularly big days when there were a great many beaters, his Lordship sometimes rolled gently off his chair after the twenty-fifth beater had drunk his health.

WHAT'S IN A NAME?

ESSEX, 1893

An Essex keeper out one day with a group of very distinguished shooting guests had just rounded them up at the end of a successful drive in which the shoot owner's dogs – worked by the keeper – had successfully collected all the birds, even the apparently inaccessible ones and a couple that no one had noticed had even been shot. A visiting lord was so impressed that he pointed to the biggest of the three dogs and shouted across to the keeper: 'What's the name of that dog?'

'I know,' came the keeper's reply.

'I dare say you do, you impudent man,' came the lord's riposte. 'Or I shouldn't have asked.'

'What about that spotty one,' he tried again. 'What's his name?'

'You know,' came the exasperating reply.

'If I did I damn well shouldn't have asked,' said the lord who then, turning to a fellow guest said, 'I can see I'll have to knock this fellow's head off for his cheek if I don't get a satisfactory answer soon.' He decided to try again as the keeper had a third dog.

'What about him? Yes, the one nearest you now?'

'Axum,' came the infuriating reply.

'Damn me if I don't get you turned out of your place for this infernal insolence,' said the lord, who was now in such a rage that he had to be restrained from hitting the keeper.

But when the owner of the shoot, who also owned the

keeper's three dogs, turned up he laughed long and loud on hearing his distinguished guest's complaint.

'I don't think you quite understand,' he said. 'Old Joe wasn't being in the least bit rude. In fact I am entirely to blame because the dogs' names are I No, U No and Axum.'

Apparently the shoot owner had been enjoying his little joke for years and no doubt the keeper enjoyed the chance to trick the occasional overbearing visitor with a joke that got better with age.

THE BARREN ROCK TOP

SCOTLAND, 1894

The late nineteenth century spawned a number of huntin', shootin' and fishin' types who devoted virtually every waking minute to sport, a word which, at that time and until well into the twentieth century was never used to describe football, cricket, rugby, etc. No, to the Victorian sportsman these were mere hobbies and pastimes. Sport meant fieldsports, the preserve of the gentleman.

The extent to which shooting could take over a man's life may be seen in the example of the Duke of Atholl, who tended to see everything in terms of sport of one kind or another.

At one of his numerous properties he'd long been irritated by some inaccessible rock formations that towered a short distance from but above the house. It was just their barrenness that irked him and despite the assurances of his men that 'Nothing had seeded up there in the memory o' man' he was often heard to mumble: 'There must be a way. I'll get some green growing up there if it's the last thing I damn well do.'

The duke travelled widely across Britain in search of shooting: he shot his own grouse, he shot deer in Scotland and he travelled south to shoot his friends' grouse and yet further south to shoot pheasants.

For years the barren scar above his land played on his mind. Then one day while shooting some particularly high pheasants he hit upon an idea for a shoot that would solve the problem of the barren rock top.

He bought some old cannon that had been used to ornament the front of an ancient and now derelict house nearby, carefully developed and tested a number of metal balls that he had specially made and then filled with the seeds of all his favourite hardy plants. On the appointed day he lined his cannon up, loaded them, took aim and fired. Great chunks of the cliff above came crashing down and Atholl and his men had to dash for cover, but the duke was delighted with the whole thing, so much so that he made it something of a regular event.

And within a year or so the cracks and holes in the barren outcrop sprouted a healthy crop of green.

CHEEKY KEEPER

SHROPSHIRE, 1895

It's worth remembering that driven shooting is a relatively modern business. Until the middle decades of the nineteenth century a man would simply go out and walk till his dog put up a bird or two. When pheasants began to be driven over a line of guns some rather more elderly gentlemen forgot, in their excitement, the basic rules, and accidents were common. Word soon got about and the more dangerous shots were placed carefully so that they could do as little harm as possible. It had to be done this way because no keeper or beater could ever suggest that a gentleman was anything less than an excellent and sporting shot. If he did he would almost certainly be sacked on the spot and once he'd been sacked he would be blacklisted and no other landowner would employ him.

Occasionally however, a keeper was so valued that he could get away with it. One keeper on a shoot in Shropshire in the 1890s was told by his employer that he, the keeper, was in charge on the shoot and that if anyone misbehaved or took a dangerous shot, the keeper should tell him so. Word spread and this particular shoot became famous as a place where the rules were applied strictly and indeed it was shoots like this that established the strict rules of etiquette that now apply on all driven shoots.

The keeper's put-downs became famous, but he could be wonderfully discreet when he liked a man.

Towards the end of his working life he was out with a party

of guns that included several dukes and two lords. A plain Mr enquired of the keeper: 'Who is that on my right?'

'Lord A—, sir,' came the keeper's reply.

'Just go and tell him where I am,' said the slightly nervous gun, knowing this particular gentleman's reputation for wild shooting.

'Beg pardon, sir, I'd rather not,' said the keeper, touching his hat. 'His Lordship always fires when he sees anything move.'

HAPSBURG RECORD

CZECHOSLOVAKIA, 1896

The Hapsburg King Carol, shooting at his huge estate at Zidlochovice in what is now the Czech Republic in the 1890s, once killed in a single day 833 pheasants. He used three guns and a team of three loaders and beaters. Even if he was an incredibly good shot – and the evidence suggests he was – on that day he must have fired something in the region of fifteen hundred cartridges in just six hours.

ESCAPE BY BIKE

AFRICA, 1897

One morning in August a shooting man living in Africa went by bicycle to visit a friend some miles away. He took his gun and strapped it to the handlebars of his bicycle, as he and his friend normally went out for a few hours bird shooting. It was just getting light as he set out and the road, which he knew well, was soft and in places muddy after recent rain. He'd just reached a steepish hill and, feeling he wasn't quite up to pedalling to the top, he dismounted and began to walk. Halfway up the hill he glanced behind him to enjoy the view across the plain when he saw a big male lion standing broadside on to him, but with its head turned in his direction.

At the very moment he spotted the lion it sprang towards him. In his fright he fell over his bicycle while trying to mount it. It was only at the third attempt that he managed to get into the saddle and even then he half sank into the soft sand of the road and wobbled violently from side to side. He began to pedal like a demented thing, but when he looked round the lion had halved the original distance between them and he was still fifty yards from the top of the hill.

The lion's growling seemed to grow louder by the second and the man's lungs felt as if they would burst, but he reached the crest of the hill just yards ahead of the lion. Almost overwhelmed by feelings of relief he tore down the other side of the hill, but elation turned to horror when he remembered that there was a ditch at the bottom of the slope. But it was too late and too dangerous now to stop. Luckily, though it was a two-foot drop into the ditch, the opposite bank was much shallower.

A moment later and he slammed down into it. He was thrown up from the saddle but in some extraordinary way managed to land back in it and continue on his way. The bicycle's forks were bent and the front wheel slightly buckled, but not so badly that he could not continue. With the adrenalin surging through his veins he reached a stretch of better-made road and sailed on towards his friend's house. When he last looked back the lion had stopped and simply stared at him as he disappeared into the distance.

A MISTY NEAR MISS

NORFOLK, 1897

The punt gunners of old worked mostly along the coast of East Anglia. All along the coast of Essex, Suffolk and Norfolk up to the Wash these professional gunners would work the streams, creeks and inlets where overwintering duck and geese would come to feed.

The gunners' punts were and are (a few are still used) canoelike, but much longer and designed to sit as low in the water as possible. The gunner would lie face down in the punt with his massive punt gun running from the centre of the punt forward, right along the bow, to project a foot or more out over the end of the boat and just above the water. A tiny scull in each hand would be used gradually to manoeuvre the punt within range and then the massive gun would be fired. The idea was to bring down as many birds as possible, for the punt gunners of old were not interested in sport; this was how they made their living and it was a precarious one.

Towards the end of the great days of punt gunning a few public-schoolboy amateurs – like Sir Peter Scott – took up the sport, but it was very different by then. The old gunners had learned the craft from their fathers and had an almost instinctive sense of where the birds would be. They also knew just how dangerous it could be if a sea fog came down or a storm. To survive a lifetime's punt gunning you needed the sixth sense of the gunner born to his trade for the punt, designed for stealth and hunting not for seaworthiness, was unforgiving in difficult conditions. Even the best of the professional punt gunners did occasionally vanish and there were near misses, as one old man recalled in 1897. He and a companion gunner had gone out on a high tide knowing that a large party of grey geese had recently arrived.

The two men decided to work their way slowly towards where they thought the birds were, each in their separate punts but always keeping an eye out for the other. When the old man gave the signal they would fire their guns.

'Pull when I flash a match,' said the old man, 'and not before.'

The old man then explained what had happened.

'All went well at first, but we got separated in the end of it, but I knew he must be pretty close by all the while, as I could sense the line of the sand and I could hear the geese talking at the edge of it. There they sat, gabbling and splashing, though I couldn't quite see them. Then I made out a body of them to the right, so I backed my paddle and looked along my big gun to see how to take them. They seemed a bit too quiet for geese. Then I thought maybe it was a piece of wreck, but I couldn't see any break in the line of it. But I saw it move so I thought to myself, here goes, and got ready to fire. Then part of a cloud cleared off from the moon and there lay his punt with him in it. Another two seconds and I should have killed or sunk him. But for the cloud there's no doubt I would have fired. Instead I backed my other paddle, backed away and breathed a sigh. I never had such a close thing.'

IN THE LION'S MOUTH

TRANSVAAL, SOUTH AFRICA, 1898

Big-game shooting did occasionally result in death for the man with the gun rather than the animals in his sights and there are many extraordinary stories of narrow escapes. One of the most extraordinary happened to a professional game ranger who worked for many years in the Transvaal region of South Africa.

The ranger was travelling home on horseback along a narrow footpath through dense bush. He was well ahead of the rest of the party who'd enjoyed a long but tiring day's shooting. The ranger wanted to get back to camp first to ensure everything was ready for his guests. As he trotted along, his dog, which had been running quietly at the heels of his horse, began to bark and whine, a mixture of aggression and fear that made the ranger realise that whatever scent the dog had picked up it was not from something insignificant.

The ranger thought they'd probably stumbled across a party of reedbucks, but the instant the thought occurred to him he spotted a big male lion crouched and half hidden on his offside.

Instinctively the ranger turned his horse away, which probably caused the lion to mistime its spring. Nonetheless, the lion managed to get its front paws on to the horse's hindquarters for an instant. The horse reared and the ranger was thrown to the ground. The horse galloped off with the lion in hot pursuit, but in the very instant the ranger thought the danger had passed, if not for his horse then at least for him, he saw another lion coming at him from the opposite direction.

The second lion trotted over to the ranger and picked him up in such a way that he was face up with his legs and body dragging beneath the body of the lion.

The lion dragged the ranger some two hundred yards along the path uttering a continual low growl. Despite some loss of blood the ranger kept his wits about him at least enough to remember that he still had his sheath knife attached to his belt on the right hip. He reached behind him with his left hand – a manoeuvre he later described as virtually impossible under normal conditions – and managed to get the knife in his hand.

Meanwhile the lion had continued to drag him until the large exposed roots of a tree stopped him temporarily. Immediately the ranger stabbed the lion twice in the side with his left hand. The lion dropped him, but stood its ground. In a frenzied lunge the ranger stabbed the lion in the throat and was instantly drenched in blood. The lion jumped back and stood three yards away, glowering and growling. The ranger, by this time soaked with his own blood and with that of the lion, scrambled to his feet. Seconds later the lion turned and went slowly away still growling. The ranger shinned up the nearest tree as fast as he could with his arm and shoulder badly mauled.

As soon as he'd made himself comfortable the first lion, having failed to catch the horse, returned. The ranger shouted to his dog who alternately barked at then dodged away from the continually charging lion. Eventually, and no doubt exhausted, the lion gave up. The ranger made it back to camp with the help of the rest of the party who by now had arrived at the scene. Next morning the stabbed lion was found dead just a few yards from the path.

ONE IN A MILLION

NORTHUMBERLAND, 1899

Shooting, like fishing and golf, lends itself to remarkable coincidences. Birds that seem to be half a mile high are brought down by a fluke shot that brings a round of applause much as, in golf, a hole in one invariably delights the crowd.

But there can be few more extraordinary flukes than that enjoyed by a gentleman farmer from Hexham, Northumberland. He'd shot the moors around the town for many years and knew all the best places, the location of which he kept a closely guarded secret.

One icy but bright afternoon he decided to end his shooting day at the best place of all – a little patch of cover by the side of a stream, a tributary of the Tyne.

Arriving at the place, the man saw a covey of partridges on the other bank of the stream but very close to the water's edge. The stream was about forty feet wide so the birds were well within range.

He crept down to the river's edge and then, gun at the ready, he stood up. The covey rose as one from the ground and he fired both barrels at once. Just as he pulled the trigger two salmon jumped from the stream. The shooter was so startled he fell over, landing on a hare, which his weight crushed to death. Some of the shot from the two barrels had killed both the salmon, the rest had accounted for five of the partridges in the covey. One shot had bagged five birds, two salmon and a hare.

172

THE GENIUS OF HYENAS

AFRICA, 1900

It is one of the truisms of nature that animals, despite all we know about them and despite how predictable we think they are, can still surprise.

When Stewart Edward White crossed Africa in 1900 in search of danger, elephants and ivory (probably in that order), he had the sense to record many of his more unusual experiences. Many of these are straight descriptions of the thousands of animals he shot, but it was the things he saw while shooting that really captured his imagination.

While bird hunting one day with a party of local beaters, he reached a broad river where the party decided to stop for lunch. While they lounged about under some trees White noticed a group of hyenas trotting briskly across the open plain towards the river. Knowing that the river was absolutely alive with crocodiles he wondered if the hyenas would try to get across and, if they did, how many would survive those gaping and very hungry crocodile jaws.

The pack of hyenas was large – there were probably twenty individuals – and when they reached the river bank they milled around aimlessly for a while almost as if they were discussing what to do. Some drank carefully, but it was clear that the drinkers, knowing just what was in the river, were extremely nervous – the least cry from a bird in the tree tops made them jump back as if electrified. Clearly the crocodiles' reputation had spread far and wide.

Two or three minutes after the hyenas had gathered at the water's edge they began to bark and howl as if their lives depended on it. White was baffled. He could see nothing that could have irritated or frightened them, but then something very strange happened. The river in front of the group of yapping hyenas began to boil and it was clear that dozens of the river crocodiles had heard all the commotion and were waiting for the hyenas to try to cross the river so they, the crocs, could enjoy an easy meal.

The yapping and howling continued and if anything increased in volume over the next few minutes. Then, as if at a signal, the hyenas ran quickly along the bank of the river for a distance of about three hundred yards. Here they stopped and immediately set up their yells and howls again.

The noise clearly carried back to where the crocodiles had gathered and immediately they too began to race upstream to the hyenas' new position. White noticed the massive size of the bow waves the crocodiles created as they put all their energies into catching up with the hyenas.

As soon as the crocodiles arrived at the hyenas' new position the noisy dogs stopped barking, raced back down the river to their original position and immediately swam across the river. So far as White could see, every hyena got across safely while twenty or thirty crocodiles milled about in the water three hundred yards downstream.

THE GROUSE'S REVENGE

YORKSHIRE, 1900

Big-game shooting often gave the quarry a genuine sporting chance of turning the tables on the shooter. Many are the tales of Victorian sportsmen waving goodbye to their wives before setting off for a day's sport in the bush only to be found in small pieces – and not very many small pieces at that – several weeks later.

Small birds are, of course, never likely to be in such a strong position as the average lion or rhino, but every now and then chance and bizarre circumstances produce a sporting bird determined to get its own back.

Richard Erskine-Hill, a wildly enthusiastic game shooter, learned the hard way that grouse shooting isn't all plain sailing.

It was his first ever day in the grouse butts and, still in his teens, he was eager to do well or at least not disgrace himself in front of the other guns. The unnerving thing about driven shooting is the waiting and it is easy to imagine Erskine-Hill's nervous excitement as he watched the faint horizon of distant purple hills that warm August morning more than a century ago.

Then he heard a faint whistle. He loaded. The tension kept mounting. Far to the south he could see tiny white specks. The beaters had started. The waiting for something to happen was almost unbearable.

Then thirty yards in front of him, he saw two big ears, a pair of whiskers and two black eyes staring at him. The hare was sitting on its haunches and it looked so comical he couldn't help but laugh.

He was still laughing when he heard two shots away to his left. He looked round and two grouse whirred over his head. They were going like bullets and he hadn't even lifted his gun.

After that he tried hard to concentrate and look to his front, but nothing more came his way for several minutes. It must have been agony not to look to left and right because he could hear guns going off everywhere, but he knew that the instant he looked to left or right he'd miss a bird coming his way.

Then he saw two black specks. They were coming straight at him. He fired and knew he'd shot his first driven grouse. He half turned to fire his second barrel at the second bird when something hit him so hard on the left side of his face that it knocked him clean off his feet.

He was certainly unconscious for several moments, but then he picked himself up, shook his head and immediately noticed blood pouring on to the barrels of his gun. He put his hand to his face, which was covered with blood. He unloaded his gun and fumbled for his handkerchief. What on earth had happened? Had he been shot?

By this time his whole face was beginning to swell and his left eye had completely closed.

The shooting slowly died down and his neighbour hurried over to see what was wrong.

'My dear boy what have you done? Have you shot yourself? That's a nasty looking eye. You'll have to have it stitched.'

Soon they were all crowding round. Then out of his right eye he saw one of his fellow guns smiling broadly. The man stooped down in the butt and picked up a grouse.

'Here's the culprit!' he announced.

The bird Erskine-Hill had hit had hit him back. When it crashed into him its sheer momentum had been enough to knock Erskine-Hill out and badly gash the left side of his face.

The local doctor said he'd been very lucky: 'Half an inch lower and you'd have lost your eye.'

HUMAN TARGET PRACTICE

ENGLAND, 1900

A correspondent writing to the *Sporting Gazette* in 1900 submitted a series of impassioned letters describing his experiments in the shooting field. He'd noticed over a number of seasons that his beaters were occasionally hit by stray shot. If the shot simply fell out of the sky (coming down with the aid of gravity following a shot at a high bird) it pattered like rain on the beater's back and head and did no harm. But at 150 yards a shot that hit a man having come straight from the muzzle of a gun could take an eye out and would get into your skin through several layers of clothing.

The *Gazette*'s correspondent described a day when he conducted a series of experiments – in a way that now seems foolhardy to the point of madness – into the relative defensive merits of different types of clothing.

First he laid out different thicknesses of a number of different cloths; tweed, wool, moleskin and cord. He put these on in varying combination and then got his servant to fire different shot sizes at him at distances of 120–150 yards.

'It was perfectly safe,' he told his readers in the *Gazette*, 'as I told my servant to be sure to fire only at my legs and besides it was nothing to what the men had to endure in the Crimea.'

At the end of the day he was quite badly hurt with blood streaming down his legs and dozens of nasty wounds but, delighted with his experiment, he announced that for maximum protection in the field several thick pairs of corduroys were probably best.

MANY PEASANTS, FEW HARES

SWEDEN, 1900

It is difficult to imagine now how different Europe was just eighty or ninety years ago. Before the Second World War quiet, forgotten communities of peasants still existed in every country from Sweden to Greece. And these were real peasants, living off the land, son taking over from father, generation after generation and usually utterly illiterate.

In England the real peasantry died out much earlier and so the attitude of foreign aristocrats must occasionally have astonished the English, who'd had a little longer to get used to the idea that the poor were also human.

Sweden, a country now famous for its liberal attitudes, was a remarkably backward place at the beginning of the twentieth century. It was still a place where – as in Russia – serfdom had only recently disappeared. The peasantry were regarded as so backward that, when it came to matters of life and death, they scarcely mattered.

This could lead to moments of great confusion and misunderstanding as when an English aristocrat, shooting as a guest at one of Sweden's most famous old estates, saw a hare coming towards him but decided not to shoot it: the beaters were already in view and he judged that the shot would not be entirely safe.

'Why did you not try for that splendid hare?' asked the Englishman's host at the end of the day.

'It was a close run thing I admit,' came the reply, 'but on

balance I thought the beaters a little too near for comfort.'

'You must not worry about these things,' said the host, 'in Sweden we have many peasants, but few hares.'

PUTTING ON THE RITZ

LONDON, 1900

Until well into the twentieth century it was quite common to see people on trains and buses carrying shotguns. Even in town a man carrying a shotgun case would arouse no comment at all and in rural districts all sorts of people carried guns – in bags and cases and out of them – on local buses. Partly this had to do with the fact that when fewer people had cars those who wanted to shoot still had to travel and partly it had to do with the sense that shotguns were not seen as a threat; they were seen as an item of sporting equipment, like a tennis racquet, or as a tool of the countryman.

In big London hotels, particularly in August, a man with several shotguns under his arm would probably be assumed to be an American on the first leg of a grouse shooting visit, but of course if a gun in a London hotel aroused no interest the same was not true once that gun was fired.

An American visitor to the Ritz in 1900 had all the shooting equipment associated with the very rich – a pair of London guns, the very best shooting clothing and two very expensive-looking and well trained dogs. But their owner was from a very rural part of the United States where a man could pretty much walk out the back door of his house and shoot whatever he liked, so when the American visitor noticed small parties of geese and duck flying over the hotel each morning and evening he thought that trying to shoot them was the most natural thing in the world.

Whether he bribed a porter or just managed to find his way to the hotel's rooftop by sheer good luck we don't know, but he was certainly crouching there the following evening and when the first party of duck flew over he managed to get two shots off at them before they veered away and dived for cover.

That first evening he fired two shots and missed both times, but he thought he had the measure of the thing and was convinced he'd have more luck the following evening. As it turned out he was right. With his first shot he downed a mallard that landed on the embankment behind the hotel. It is easy to imagine the excited American running down the stairs and out into the street and then asking the first passer-by if he or she had happened to see a duck fall out of the sky.

The American carried on shooting each evening for five days before an elderly hotel guest complained about the terrible noise each evening from the roof. The management had no idea what the guest was talking about but they sent someone up the following evening and he discovered what was going on. The hotel's reaction to these unusual goings-on is not recorded, but the shooting stopped and the American was soon on his way to Yorkshire. The hotel management probably had no objection to the shooting itself, only perhaps to the noise and the disturbance of the other guests.

SNIPE COINCIDENCE

NORFOLK, 1900

A Mr Shaw and his son regularly went shooting for snipe along the banks of the tidal River Ouse in Norfolk. One Saturday they decided to set off a little earlier than usual but without their dog, which had injured its leg on a previous outing.

After a couple of hours during which nothing happened (but they had a long talk about various matters and enjoyed the sight of geese flighting way out across the estuary) they turned for home. Part of their return journey took them close alongside the muddiest part of the tidal Ouse and it was as they wandered along this part of the river that the elder Mr Shaw spotted a snipe and shot it. The bird fell, apparently dead, but well out on the deepest part of the mud.

Neither father nor son thought it was worth ploughing through thigh deep mud for one small snipe so they left it where it had fallen and continued on their way home. Between the spot where the bird was shot and the house where the Shaws lived was just over a mile and the distance was entirely taken up by parkland.

Having crossed the park the two men reached their house and found Mrs Shaw standing on the drive with her daughter. The two were just in the process of examining a dead snipe. They explained that a few moments earlier they'd heard a fluttering in the trees above the drive. Then, right at their feet fell the snipe. The snipe had mud on its breast and under its wings – unmistakably mud from the river.

The question was – could this possibly be the bird that had been shot and left in the mud of the tidal river a mile away?

The younger Mr Shaw immediately set off back to the river and to the spot where the bird had fallen – he found the bird had gone. The bird that had fallen from the trees in the drive was the same bird that had been left for dead. It had obviously recovered sufficiently to overtake father and son on their way home, before dropping just ten feet from their front door.

SPIDER SHOOTING

YORKSHIRE, 1900

It was a glorious day for grouse shooting, which, of course, it always should be on the twelfth of August, the day the season opens. The keepers agreed the grouse had enjoyed one of the most successful breeding seasons for years and there were plenty of strong birds for the party of distinguished guns.

A carriage waited to take the early birds to the station and then on by express train to London where they would be eaten that very evening. The keepers agreed this was a bit of fun – this rushing the first grouse to London – but they also agreed that without hanging till the maggots were dropping out of it, the first grouse would be a pretty tasteless specimen.

The party of guns was distinguished in the sense that they were rich and well connected, but they were elderly. Several had sticks, one had two sticks and, the keepers knew from experience, one particularly elderly banker was extremely short-sighted. He didn't shoot particularly well because of his eyes, but at least he was safe and didn't need to be led about like a child like some of these old buffers. Privately, anyway, that was the keepers' view.

The morning went well. The grouse flew like supersonic jets, the guns did reasonably well given their general level of infirmity and everyone seemed to be enjoying themselves – everyone that is except the elderly banker. He'd been strangely quiet at first, hardly lifting his gun to the first few birds that came his way. Was he confused or ill perhaps? The keepers

184

were too polite to ask, but they kept an eye on him.

An hour before lunch he began blasting off like a maniac, firing both barrels, reloading immediately and firing again. In between shots he shouted, 'Mark that bird. He's definitely hit.' Then there would be a pause of several minutes before another rapid burst of firing. 'That bird has a leg down. Damn – winged him,' and so on.

The keepers were baffled. It was mostly during the pauses between shooting that the birds passed over the old banker and when he did start shooting there was usually nothing in the air. When the birds appeared and he fired at the right time he was clearly not shooting in the right direction anyway.

They delicately asked him at lunch if they could get him anything, but he said he was fine. It was only later that the explanation for his extraordinary behaviour filtered back via several other guns who roared with laughter when they told each other the tale.

At some stage in the proceedings a spider had attached itself to the peak of the old man's hat. It had then lowered itself from a thread until it was suspended in front of his right eye. Every time he caught sight of it he assumed it was a grouse and started firing at it.

THE HONEST POACHER

LINCOLNSHIRE, 1901

Latimer Lee, or Blucher as he was generally known, was a famous Lincolnshire poacher who died in 1905. In his long career – he'd started poaching while at school in the 1840s – he had taken countless thousands of pheasants from local estates and was the bane of every keeper for miles around. He had the usual silent poacher's dog – an animal trained from the very first never ever to bark whatever the provocation – but Latimer's dog was cleverer than the average and when the old poacher was looking for birds the dog would range well ahead of him searching for the first signs of danger either in the form of the police or a keeper. If the dog sensed anyone was there it would race back to Latimer and put its head in his hand. That was the danger signal and it meant Latimer knew well in advance that trouble was brewing and it was time to go home.

Despite the fact that just about everyone knew that Latimer Lee was a poacher he had a reputation as a man of complete honesty. In every sphere of life other than game finding he never dreamed of cheating. Ironically it was this reputation that once stood him in good stead in court. He'd been out poaching and had successfully caught half a dozen pheasants, which were safely hung up in his shed. Then walking into Grantham with a friend, he stopped to collect a big bag of onions. As they reached the town they met a policeman who promptly arrested them.

Next day they were up in court for stealing the onions. Now

the policeman was new to the area and, knowing Blucher's reputation as a poacher, he simply assumed that pretty much everything the man did was probably illegal.

But Blucher's attitude in the dock and his speech convinced the magistrate immediately of his innocence.

'Stealing onions!' he gasped. 'Stealing onions! Why, I'd scorn to do such a thing. You all know what my business is. I'm a poacher. I wouldn't lower myself to onions!'

The case was dismissed.

VANISHING FAMILY

FRANCE, 1902

By the end of the nineteenth century France had become a fashionable resort for Englishmen – particularly younger Englishmen – of means. The attraction was precisely those qualities reviled in the English newspapers. France was dangerously fast, its women's morals questionable, its addiction to pleasure disgraceful. So, from Le Touquet to Cannes the sons of old and new money left stuffy old England in search of adventure. France was not much thought of as a sporting destination. Although the authorities kept French woodland plentifully stocked with wild boar for *la chasse*, the English were more interested in organised bird shooting, which was something the French simply did not have. They preferred to walk several miles in a pursuit of, say, a single duck or goose.

However, the English love of shooting was well known and wherever young tourists alighted from French trains with guns in their baggage, local guides would be sure to pop up out of nowhere and offer to show them the best sport in the region. Often the plan by the French guides was simply to jolly the Englishman along until the opportunity arose to steal his gunpowder – there seemed always to be a shortage in France and English powder had a worldwide reputation.

In one such incident a young man, fresh down from Cambridge and on the brink of a distinguished career at the bar, met a whole family of French peasants as he clattered

188

along the platform with fifteen or sixteen porters in attendance and four tons of boxes, bags and suitcases. 'They were absolutely charming,' the Englishman later declared, 'although I couldn't understand much of their regional French.'

Somehow they persuaded the young man to visit them in some mountainous region of the Pyrenees with the promise of fine shooting and the best guides in the country. The Englishman turned up at their tiny hillside hovel intending to stay for a few days before returning to his hotel, and, leaving two of his best guns in the house along with a great deal of his other luggage, set off with one gun and the minimum required for a day's shooting. The youngest son was to be his guide and the Englishman was in high spirits after listening to endless tales of the number and quality of the birds he would certainly encounter.

By lunchtime they'd succeeded only in being chased by an extremely angry bear, which seemed far more terrifying to the local guide than to the Englishman. They stopped for lunch and after enjoying a bottle of his guide's home-made wine the Englishman fell asleep. When he woke his guide was nowhere to be seen. He searched everywhere but the guide had vanished and it was with great difficulty and a deal of luck that the Englishman managed to find his way back to the French family's tiny mountain house. When he arrived three hours later and more than a little angry he pushed the door open only to discover that the house was empty – not a stick of furniture remained and his precious guns and other luggage had gone with them. They were never seen again.

CROCODILE RIDING

INDIA, 1903

Though they felt no compunction about slaughtering every animal they encountered, our sporting ancestors were also great natural historians. No detail of a creature's plumage, behaviour or habit was too trivial to be noted down and usually at great length. Game books were not complete if they did not contain, pinned to the page, an unusual pheasant beak, a six-toed pheasant foot or whatever.

Many sportsmen loved the idea of publishing books about their experiences across the world and these too are often fascinating records of the natural history and habits of now rare or protected animals. ˙

One anonymous author who lived for many years in India accounted for dozens of tigers, bears and little-known species of deer and antelope. He seems to have had a particular fascination with the contents of the stomachs of the animals he shot. He was also completely fearless when it came to running in after wounded game, believing that no gentleman would knowingly leave a wounded animal in the bush. But of course if a tiger is dangerous under normal circumstances it is absolutely deadly when injured and our anonymous hero had several near misses, coming away with torn limbs and, once, a badly mauled shoulder. He always said he was happiest shooting crocodiles and alligators ('a hippo is decidedly not worth bothering,' he once said, 'just a great watery bladder.').

On one crocodile hunting trip he shot a particularly big

specimen from a boat in the middle of the river and, when he thought it was in danger of drifting away or sinking out of sight, he jumped on its back and waited for his beaters to throw a line to him so man and croc could be brought to shore.

Immediately it was dragged up the beach our sportsman cut it open and noted the contents of its stomach: astonishingly that one crocodile contained a small wooden chest, a wallet (with money still in it), a human skull, a corkscrew, a soda-water bottle, a number of railway tickets, a tobacco pouch (with tobacco still in it), some brass candlesticks, a tin box and, for good measure, a whole calf.

.

SNAKE LASSO

INDIA, 1903

Of all the animals that shooting men have pursued the python has to be among the strangest, but with the mania for collecting for institutions like the Natural History Museum the python hunt was an occasional occurrence.

When a natural history museum in America needed a python they called on the services of the governor of what was then known as the United Provinces of India.

He in turn employed a local jungle expert who knew of an absolutely enormous specimen that lived along a certain stretch of the local river. To avoid damaging the python with gunshot a small group of hunters was put together to try to lasso the beast, which was at least eighteen feet long. The hunter stayed alongside with his gun at the ready in case anything went seriously wrong, but he knew that he would not be popular with the authorities if he shot the python.

The hunters spotted the python lying half on a log in the river and half in the water. Three men approached the giant snake, each with a lasso on the end of a long piece of rope. The plan was to get a noose round each end of the animal simultaneously. When they were within ten feet the snake lifted its head, slithered into the water and headed straight for the nearest man. Having scared the living daylights out of the hunting party the python vanished beneath the roots of a half-sunk tree.

A few days later an even bigger party of huntsmen decided

to try again, for it was known that a python, with so few enemies, is extremely territorial staying from birth to death in the same few yards of river. They were very unlikely ever again to get the chance to catch such a big specimen.

Back at the river all went well as the men with ropes entered the water. The python appeared to be fast asleep on his log just as before but with two-thirds of his great length hidden beneath the water.

As the first hunter came close to slipping the noose over the python's head there was a swirl a little downstream of the python's head and then in an instant the hunter with the noose nearest the snake's head vanished as if pulled under by a giant hand. The other men with the ropes dashed out of the water while the hunter fired repeatedly at the place where the snake had been seconds before.

They dragged the river for the rest of that day but nothing could be found. The following day they returned once more and combed the banks looking for a sighting of the great snake. Again nothing. On the third day when they reached the river the snake lay dead half in and half out of the water, but this time its great head lay up a shallow muddy bank.

They dragged the massively bloated animal out of the water and noticed deep bite marks on either side of its head. An expert naturalist confirmed that the python had probably been killed by otters which, despite having no desire to eat snake, will occasionally attack even the biggest python. Their technique was to approach the snake one on either side of its head. No otter would ever attack a snake on its own. It could only be achieved if it was a team effort. When the snake moved to attack the first otter its mate on the snake's blind side would nip in quickly and take a bite out of the python's head. When the snake turned to attack this otter, the other would move in quickly and take a bite out of the other side of the snake just behind the head. After four or five such manoeuvres back and forth the snake would succumb from loss of blood.

It looked as if this is what had happened to the massive snake that the hunters had tried to lasso, but a further surprise was in store for the men who carried the snake up on to an elephant's back so it could be carried back to the village. When the python was taken down it was decided that, as the skin was already damaged by the bites taken from its neck, there was no point in treating it with particular care. The hunters thought they would keep just the skin so they proceeded to cut the great snake open. Inside was the body of the Indian who had tried to lasso the animal's head. He was still fully clothed and had hardly been digested at all – clearly the otters, or whatever had killed the snake, got there soon after the man vanished into the river.

PHEASANT KILLS HARE

CAPENOCH, 1904

Perhaps the most extraordinary coincidence in the shooting field occurred at Capenoch in Scotland one blustery day in 1904. A team of gentleman Scots – who actually sounded more English than the English but were blessed with names like MacDonald and MacGregor – were shooting pheasants. They'd had a good morning. Few pheasants had come their way but those they'd seen were high, wild birds, the sort every shooting man dreams of. The men had agreed that for safety reasons they wouldn't shoot ground game – rabbits and hares – during the morning and they decided over lunch that although they'd seen plenty of rabbits they would stick to their rule and let them go by unsaluted that afternoon.

The friends were walking up pheasants rather than waiting for them to be driven over them, so they were particularly surprised when a big cock pheasant got up well ahead of them – well out of range – and then climbed high into the sky before turning to fly back over the guns. It soared well over to the left of the group of friends but for the man on the left it was certainly an acceptable distance for a shot. He duly fired and the pheasant came tumbling out of the sky. Just at that moment a hare ran past and out across the wide pasture behind them. Halfway across the pasture the astonished guns watched as the pheasant crashed into the running hare, killing it stone dead.

BANDIT ATTACK

CORSICA, 1905

A Scotsman living in Italy on an estate he'd bought with a fortune made in shipping was out shooting one day for partridges with his son. They were returning from a successful day when the son felt a bullet smash into the rock outcrop against which he'd stopped for a short rest.

Seeing no one around the son shouted out in Corsican, saying he was a hunter and meant no one any harm. The only reply was a second bullet, which whistled close by again. A third bullet hit the young man's father in the head, but as the father later said a Scottish head is a wonderful thing and it would take more than a bullet fired from a Winchester at two hundred yards to do it any damage.

The father and son took cover immediately but whenever they peeped above the parapet another bullet whistled by. In all, eight shots were fired before the two managed to get far enough away to make further shooting pointless, and all the shooting had taken place within a few hundred yards of a main road.

The two men discovered later that Paoli, a famous bandit, occupied a cave in the hill just above the spot where the two men had stopped to rest. When the police arrived back on the scene Paoli's cave was located and surrounded. The Scotsman and his son stood by, amused and curious as to the outcome. The police decided that a direct advance on the cave was too dangerous, as they did not know how many bandits were in the cave nor how well they were armed.

The police decided the only way was to set fire to the bush surrounding the cave. When it had completely burned out the police advanced, hoping no doubt to find the charred remains of Paoli and his confederates. To their fury they discovered that the bandits had long gone and all their efforts were in vain, but for the two Scotsmen the day's shooting had turned into something far more exciting.

Indeed the two men discovered later that Paoli had another cave a little higher up the mountain from which he looked down, with amusement, on the whole proceedings. In any case the first cave was blown up using dynamite, no doubt to ensure that it could never again be used by Paoli or any other bandit.

Paoli, on hearing that the police were looking for him in consequence of the attack on the two Scotsmen, was apparently outraged. He denied he'd attacked them and to prove it sent the police one of his rifles to show that it was of a different bore from that used in the attack. Many theories for the attack on the sportsmen were put forward over the years: that Paoli had thought they were police in disguise and fired at them (assuming he was indeed the villain of the piece). Another theory was that he always made it a rule to shoot at anyone who might happen to come within a certain range of his hiding place. A third theory was that Paoli had just acquired a new rifle and was eager to try it out and that these two happened to come in handy for the purpose.

Shortly after the two Scotsmen escaped with their lives there was another encounter between Paoli and the police. Paoli had a very intelligent little white terrier which used to go scouting for him. By its manner when it returned Paoli could be sure whether or not there happened to be anyone in the neighbourhood. The police were naturally anxious to get the dog into custody.

One day two policemen riding along the main road happened to see the little dog. One was all for shooting it on the spot; the other suggested they wait and try to capture Paoli as well. Moments later they were shot at and were lucky to escape with their lives. Paoli's little dog had clearly needed only a few minutes to betray their whereabouts to its master.

Paoli was once captured and sent to Devil's Island but no sooner had he arrived than he discovered that his gaolers were fellow Corsicans and they quickly contrived to let him escape. The two Scotsmen went shooting over the same territory for many years and they were never shot at again. Perhaps Paoli accepted the fact that, after all, they were not policemen.

LAST OF THE PASSENGER PIGEON

NORTH AMERICA, 1906

In the 1850s in the United States the passenger pigeon was still probably the commonest animal alive. In fact it is believed that the passenger pigeon was and still is the most populous bird that has ever lived. Migrating flocks of these birds would darken the sky for weeks on end and an individual flock might take four days to pass. About the size of a woodpigeon the passenger pigeon was also a pest so it was persecuted widely. Huge numbers were shot, limed, netted and poisoned – the numbers of birds involved were so great that those killed were measured in tons.

The slaughter continued year in and year out, yet still the vast flocks seemed to pass at their usual times of migration. Young shooters learned their skills on these hard-flying but common birds that just always seemed to be there. Then suddenly they were gone and a couple of friends in a field one morning in 1906 were probably the last to shoot a few passenger pigeons. The huge flocks hadn't been seen for a decade or more and a law had been introduced to protect the few passenger pigeon the authorities hoped might remain. When the two shooters saw a few passengers in a tree and shot them they probably thought that they were the vanguard of the mighty returning flocks. In fact they were part of a flock of a few thousand and no one knew that a flock of a few thousand would not be enough to save the species, for only too late was it realised that passenger pigeon relied on flocks that were massive in order to breed. A flock of a few thousand was not big enough to trigger whatever mechanism prompted the urge to breed and so the last few passenger pigeon – including the two shot by those two men in a field in 1906 – vanished into history. The very last passenger pigeon of all died in Cincinnati Zoo in 1917.

THE POULTRY MAN

BERWICKSHIRE, 1906

Lord Home recalled a visitor to the Hirsel at Coldstream who was an enthusiastic shot. When asked if he would like to try grouse shooting he expressed interest, but was more concerned to know how big these grouse were, for he had never seen them before. Out in the butts next day the visitor was given a butt right in the middle of the drive where he would be sure to get plenty of birds. At lunch Lord Home gently enquired if his visitor had enjoyed the morning. Home was rather nervous as he had noticed that his visitor had not fired a single shot despite a continuous stream of birds.

'There was nothing to shoot,' came the man's reply. 'I saw only dozens of poultry, some kind of chicken I think they must have been.'

SPANISH CLAY SHOOTER

ISLE OF WIGHT, 1906

Shooting and fishing have perhaps uniquely retained to a large extent their class distinctions. In fishing the wealthy still fish pretty much exclusively for trout and salmon – the so-called game fish – while more humble fishermen await the attentions of the lowly perch, pike, roach, rudd and gudgeon – the so-called coarse fish.

It is the same in shooting. The wealthy shoot grouse and pheasants, the poor (or poorer) shoot pigeons and rabbits, and although there is some overlap the division retains its old hold.

Occasionally of course there are surprises, and none more so than the day in 1906 when the Isle of Wight Clay-Shooting Championships were held. Clay shooting is still pretty largely the preserve of the working man and you will not often find peers of the realm lining up at the Crafty Old Magpie stand. The same was true in 1906 and the Isle of Wight then was still relatively remote.

Local farmers and farm workers must have been curious to see an obvious foreigner with a large number of servants making his way carefully from stand to stand. What on earth was this Hercule Poirot figure doing?

All was made clear at the end of the day when the prizes were handed out. In first place was the 'fat little foreigner' as a local newspaper disrespectfully referred to him. It was only later that the fat little foreigner was discovered to be none other than the Spanish King Alphonso XIII.

TRICK-SHOOTING KING

ENGLAND, 1906

Kings were often a problem on shoots because however greedy or selfish they were – whether for lunch or sport – they could not be criticised. Things might be different now but in the nineteenth and early twentieth century the tradition of deference to one's superiors ran deep. Usually this was not a problem as kings, more perhaps than anyone, were brought up on a diet of shooting, fishing and stalking, the traditional sports – even today – of male members of royal European families.

The habit of deference occasionally produced a royal shot of unparalled eccentricity – like King Carlos of Portugal who was very short, very fat and very unpopular in his home country. So much so that he was assassinated in 1908. Before that unhappy event, he was a regular guest at many English country houses where he apparently showed all the embarrassing arrogance of what we would now describe as the tinpot dictator. He travelled always with a large retinue of staff, specially chosen it seemed for their ability to flatter the king in ways that were convincing – at least to the king. If Carlos listened to music his courtiers would whisper that it was a great pity he had not devoted his life to music, as he would certainly have been the equal of Beethoven if he had put his mind to it. When he painted a muddy little oil he was told that art had lost a great deal when God sent Carlos to earth to rule rather than wield a brush. And so on. Worst of all, the habit of hearing his modest talents praised to the skies had never been tempered by a single realistic comment and he was convinced that all of it was true. This meant that no sooner had he been told he was an accomplished skier than he told everyone else as if it were an incontrovertible fact. Modesty being one of the genuine attributes of the English gentleman, this did not go down well at all, but of course politeness demanded that he be accepted at his own value of himself.

In the shooting field things were no better. Carlos had seen an American trick shooter in action and decided (after a quiet word with a courtier or two) that he could do just as well. Thus it was that, wherever he shot, Carlos either shot from the hip or he would shoot first from one shoulder and then from the other or even occasionally from between his legs and all the while he infuriated the guns on either side of him in the line by continually singing (and rather badly) arias from his favourite operas.

FORTY WINKS

ENGLAND, 1907

The vast majority of shooting dogs love being out in the field so much that they will pick up and retrieve until they drop from exhaustion. It's in their nature since for generations they have been bred specifically for the purpose, but one dog decided it had had enough of shooting despite its impeccable pedigree.

The dog was owned by a friend of that great shooting enthusiast King Edward VII. Not wanting to be disgraced by a poor animal in such illustrious company, the king's friend had made sure that the dog came from a long line of excellent gundogs, yet on its first day in the field the dog vanished half way through the first drive. It reappeared at about lunchtime and was as good as gold until the shooting started again in the afternoon. Then it disappeared again and despite a great deal of searching it could not be found until about three o'clock when the last drive ended.

At subsequent shoots the same thing happened and the dog, once gone, could never be found. Then, finally, a beater who'd stayed well behind the other beaters after hurting his foot saw the disappearing dog creeping through the field and dropping into a nearby ditch. The beater hobbled over and found the dog curled up, fast asleep and snoring loudly. And there it slept until some sixth sense told it lunch was in the offing, at which time it woke up and headed back to its master. Nothing could be done to stop the dog's bizarre behaviour. If kept at its owner's peg it stayed alert and interested in the proceedings, but once let off to retrieve a bird it always vanished and was found, when it was found at all, curled up asleep. In the end its exasperated owner gave the dog to his mother to be kept as a pet, which is perhaps just what the dog wanted all along.

RATCATCHER

SURREY, 1908

A notorious poacher who operated in and around the Surrey town of Mitcham was stopped early one morning in 1908. He had a big sack and was walking brazenly up the high street as if he didn't care who saw him. The police pounced, convinced that at last they had caught him red-handed. He protested his innocence, saying there was nothing in the bag that could possibly interest the police. But there was something alive in the sack, the poacher had a reputation and the police were keen to nail their man. Poacher and police set off for the local police station where, after much discussion and argument, the contents of the bag were tipped out on to the floor.

Immediately the scene was one of pandemonium as nearly thirty huge rats immediately dashed for cover in every direction. The police evacuated the police station, which had to be shut down for the rest of the day.

The poacher, who'd been pursued by the police for years for illegally using his shotgun in the local woods, was in no mood to help out. He went next door to the pub, bought himself a pint and refused to budge despite all the pleas of the local police chief. It was only when, four hours later, the poacher was offered a large sum of money by the police (who'd now missed virtually a whole day's work) that he agreed to go back into the station and catch his rats. He managed the feat in less than twenty minutes and then disappeared up the high street with a big smile on his face and ten pounds in his pocket.

LIVING OFF THE LAND

IRELAND, 1909

An Edwardian schoolmaster who conceived a passion for shooting devoted his life to sport. At first he left England for the snipe bogs of Ireland every summer and seemed happy to return to his schoolmastering when the autumn term began, but gradually with each passing year he found excuses to go a few days before the summer term had properly ended and to return perhaps a few days late for the start of the autumn term. For the first two years the headmaster at his school – it was a famous public school – thought that the schoolmaster had just been unlucky with train and boat times, with the difficulties of travel in the days of steam trains and steam ships.

But when the schoolmaster left school two weeks before term ended and missed the whole of the first autumn half the headmaster decided it was time to speak to him.

'You really must try to be here until the other masters' leave – until the end of term – and you must get back in time for the new term, otherwise what am I to tell the parents?' said the head.

'Very well, I resign,' said the schoolmaster.

The head, astonished, replied: 'But you can't just resign. I need time to find a replacement and besides you cannot throw your career away like this.'

'I can and I will. I have wasted enough of my life with these half-witted boys.'

With that he packed his bags and left for Ireland, from

where he never returned. He spent the last forty years of his life in a tiny one roomed cabin on a remote moor in the west of Ireland, shooting and fishing and living entirely on what he could shoot and catch. He never saw his family again and visitors were discouraged by his increasingly eccentric ways. He made his own ammunition when his money ran out and was eventually seen running barefoot across the moor with his rusty old gun slung over his shoulders. His hair and beard grew longer, but he never lost his passion for shooting and local farmers regularly reported seeing him tramp several dozen miles a day in search of a remote loch or moor where only he knew he would find a little game.

Eventually he was found emaciated and in a state of collapse in his tiny cabin. He'd lived there for more than forty years, during which time he'd hardly spoken to a soul, but when they carried him to the town he continually mumbled, 'I must have my old gun. Where is it? Don't take me away or I will die.' And sure enough, within days of being admitted to hospital he died. His will was found in the house and in it he described his philosophy of life. 'All my days spent in the town and in civilised society were wasted. I only came alive when I came here and understood that this was the place and the life I was made for.' It was a strange end for an old Etonian, but nothing in the will suggested that he had been anything but happy in his curious exile.

ATTEMPTED MURDER

NORFOLK, 1910

Mantraps were once a common feature of the British countryside. The rights of property were paramount and a man with a starving family could justifiably be killed in one of these fearsome devices if he poached a single rabbit, even though he was probably poaching on land taken from him during the period of enclosures. Long after they were outlawed in Victoria's reign, mantraps continued to be used in out-of-the-way places, and on at least one occasion with extraordinary results.

A Norfolk keeper in about 1910 had caught the village poacher dozens of times. The man had been fined and imprisoned, but as soon as he was out he started poaching again. The keeper was at his wits' end, particularly as the poacher was an out-and-out brute who had more than once physically attacked him.

Things came to a head when the poacher threatened to murder the keeper if he ever tried to catch him again. The weeks passed and then, at the beginning of the season, the two men met at dusk in a wood. As soon as the poacher saw the keeper he put his gun to his shoulder and fired straight at him. The shot tore through the keeper's thick jacket as he dodged to one side, but missed his hip by an inch. The poacher immediately ran off.

After this, though it was against the law, the keeper decided a mantrap was the only answer. He went into an old, long-disused barn behind the big house and pulled out a massive rusty mantrap. It was about two feet in diameter with savage teeth and, when sprung, it would smash a man's leg about twelve inches up the shin. The keeper oiled it and checked it was working and then set it in a wood that he knew was a favourite of the poacher. He hid the loaded trap at a narrow gap through which he was convinced the poacher would make his way. Next morning, doing his usual rounds just after the dawn he came across the poacher, his leg stuck fast in the trap. He was clearly in a great deal of pain and, after several hours moaning and groaning on the damp ground, he'd also become feverish and disorientated.

The keeper picked up the poacher's gun and said: 'You tried to shoot me and now I've caught you. If I let you out of this you've got to keep clear of my woods and coverts. Are we agreed?' The trapped man nodded and the keeper released him from the trap. The poacher hobbled away down the track without saying a word.

The poacher lost his leg as a result of the wounds inflicted by the trap, but his days of violence and theft were over. Even his wife said he was a kinder, gentler man who stayed at home more. The poacher knew that if he'd complained to the police about the trap, the keeper would have had him arrested for attempted murder.

HEAD-BANGER

SCOTLAND, 1910

Scottish head keepers, like gillies, have always been a race apart and even the mightiest lord or earl would think twice before getting on the wrong side of such a man. Among the most famous or infamous Scottish keepers was Donald Ross. Ross was a remarkably talented man who transformed the shooting on Lord Portland's estate at Langwell and it was he who introduced the heather burning that made driven grouse shooting possible by ensuring an abundance of young shoots of heather each year – without burning there was less young heather and therefore far fewer pheasants.

Ross was only rarely intimidated by his boss and his friends however high and mighty, but he was famously subtle in his put-downs. Whenever he had to write to Lord Cole, which thankfully from Ross's point of view was not often, he would address him as 'Dear Lord Coal,' but Ross's independent spirit reached its apogee one morning in the kitchens at Langwell. Lord Portland had recently paid a great deal of money to persuade a top French chef to work for him – the fashion for French food among the English aristocracy then being at its height – but Ross disliked the culinary genius intently. All seemed harmonious enough in the weeks following the chef's arrival until one morning a group of servants heard furious shouts and screams coming from the kitchen. They rushed in to find Ross sitting on top of the terrified chef – who was sprawled across the floor – banging his head on the floor and shouting at the top of his voice 'Remember Waterloo!'

HEDGEHOG HAT

NORFOLK, 1910

The famous Victorian shot, Lord Walsingham, was also a brilliant entomologist. In between shooting specimen birds for the British Museum he found time to collect a huge range of butterflies, moths and other insects. Some of the very rarest insects were found only in remote undrained parts of the fens and it was here that Walsingham spent a great deal of his time, but particularly in that last unspoiled corner of fenland at Wicken. Wicken Fen, then as now, attracted entomologists from all over the world. As the site is now owned by the National Trust they come to look and study. In Walsingham's time they came with their nets and killing bottles to catch rarities.

When he went insect hunting or bird shooting Walsingham dressed in the most extraordinary way. He wore breeches and a huge moleskin jacket under which there gleamed his favourite snakeskin waistcoat, but most extraordinary of all was his headgear – a hat made from a large, whole hedgehog skin complete with erect spikes, its head and two artificial eyes. Walsingham wore it with the hedgehog's head coming down in the middle of his head between his eyes. The effect was to make it seem as if Walsingham had two heads – his own and then immediately above it that of a monster.

Whether he was shooting or collecting butterflies, Walsingham stayed with a man called Isaac Apsland who was an uncle of the writer James Wentworth Day. One of Apsland's favourite stories was of the day Albert Houghton, the village cobbler and another remarkable amateur entomologist, first met Lord Walsingham, who was later to become one of his closest friends.

Late one summer evening, probably in about 1910, Houghton was coming across Wicken Fen when out of the mist loomed a tall, extraordinary looking creature with a hedgehog apparently alive and well and keeping lookout on top of his head.

'Who on earth are you?' said Houghton with a look of astonishment.

'I'm a friend of Mr Apsland. In fact I'm staying with him,' came the reply.

'Get out of it,' said the shoemaker, 'Master wouldn't have a rum-looking pup like you in the house. Get on with you and don't let me catch you down the fen again or you'll be in the dyke!'

And on that note they parted. The very next morning, as Wentworth Day later recalled, Houghton called at Mr Apsland's house just after breakfast. And there, at the table, was the apparition from the previous night. Apsland made the introduction. 'Meet my good friend – who also happens to be one of the best entomologists in the world – Lord Walsingham.'

'Well, I'm damned,' said Houghton, 'if you ain't that rum old bugger I saw last night. Well how the devil was I to know who you were if you will dress up like that!'

It was an inauspicious beginning but Houghton and Walsingham were friends for life from that day.

MISSIONARY POSITION

AFRICA, 1910

While on safari in what was then British East Africa in about 1910, a British sportsman stopped at a small village and was told that a missionary had recently arrived. The sportsman hunted round the village to find his fellow countryman and on meeting him discovered he was on his way to the coast to take ship for Europe. The missionary had spent a few days in the village as he was suffering badly from malaria. He was so tired he could barely lift his own hat and lay hopelessly on a dirty bed surrounded by flies. But the missionary had some wonderful tales, one of which concerned a meeting with a lion.

The missionary had been asleep in his tent back at the mission he'd run for some years. When he went to bed he'd heard the usual nocturnal roars of the lions, but since he heard them every night he thought nothing of it. He took off his clothes, put his whip by the bed, which he did every night, blew out his oil lamp and got ready for sleep.

At the best of times he was not a good sleeper and a couple of hours later he felt restless and rolled over, at the same time opening an eye slightly. All idea of sleep vanished in an instant when he saw peering in at the door of his tent a large lioness. He immediately reached down beside the bed and grabbed what he thought was his whip. He hurled it at the lioness's head, feeling sure that this would be enough to scare her off, so having thrown his whip he rolled over and tried again to get to sleep. He was so tired by now that sleep came quickly and he was aware of nothing more until dawn came. First light was his normal time for getting up so he dressed and stepped outside the tent to see what sort of day it was. As soon as he opened the tent flap he was astonished to see, lying on the ground, the lioness stone dead. Lying beside her was a venomous snake, also dead but with its stomach torn open by the claws of the lioness.

It immediately became apparent that what he thought had been his whip in the middle of the night had actually been one of the most venomous snakes in Africa – a snake, moreover, whose venom always proved deadly since no antidote to it was known.

The missionary's snake-throwing had been so accurate that the deadly serpent had hit the lion in the eye and at that very moment the snake lashed out and pushed its fangs into a spot just below the lioness's eye. Once bitten the lion pounced in fury and tore the snake apart, by which time the poisonous venom was already beginning to do its work. The snake was already dead but within minutes the lioness too had succumbed. There is no doubt that if the missionary had not hurled the snake either the snake or the lioness would have killed him.

THE REEDBUCK THAT STOOD
ITS GROUND

AFRICA, 1910

While out shooting in the Masai lands along Africa's Kedong Valley in 1910, Stewart Edward White stood at the top of a small hill and looked about him. He later wrote that it was in that moment that he realised the incredible richness of the region's wildlife and its sheer abundance. As far as he could see great herds of oribi, steinbok, reedbuck, impala and wildebeest moved across the plain and wherever he and his men moved that day and the next the same vast herds could be seen everywhere round about, but always keeping a safe distance from the party of humans.

It was certainly true that the fear of man among these animals was at least as deeply imbedded in their genetic make-up as the fear of lion or leopard, but on the day he stood on that ridge White experienced something quite inexplicable; something that seemed to contradict everything he had learned about the animal kingdom. He reached a small clearing and was just in time to see the disappearing hindquarters of a small group of reedbuck. Then he noticed that they had not all gone. A single delicate reedbuck, its flanks heaving but otherwise ramrod-still stared at White, who raised his gun. He didn't want the animal for its trophy, but simply to add to that day's quota of meat, but something about its utter stillness made him uneasy. He took the gun from his shoulder and walked towards the reedbuck thinking that if it didn't bolt he really would shoot it. He was within ten paces and still the reedbuck stood its ground. White later said that he didn't shoot because close up he had been aware of every detail of the reedbuck's delicate beauty and somehow he couldn't bear to reduce the living animal to a bloodied corpse. Eventually, having got close enough to touch the animal, he simply walked past it and on out of the clearing. When he looked back a few moments later the reedbuck had gone.

THICK-HEADED BISON

INDIA, 1910

A young officer in the Indian army decided to enjoy a day's shooting just a week after arriving in India in the summer of 1910. He knew little about the local flora and fauna and even less about shooting. He wandered out into the countryside with an old lightweight black-powder rifle and its amateurish home-made bullets almost as if he was out roaming the hedgerows at home in search of an occasional pigeon.

In some ways, given what happened next, the young officer owed his life entirely to his own ignorance. He had hardly gone a mile along a track towards an outlying village when a massive bull bison stepped out into the path ahead of him about fifty yards away.

The story is a gruesome one and one almost feels more pity for the bison than relief that the soldier escaped with his life, but having seen the bull the soldier simply raised his gun and fired at it. He was an excellent shot – he was later declared the best shot in the Indian army – and his bullet struck the bison just where it should have done to ensure a good clean kill. It was, in fact, an absolutely textbook shot. But the soldier did not quite realise what it was he was dealing with, for a bison's head is immensely thick and his hide even more so. The bullet seemed merely to irritate the animal. It shook its head, lowered its horns and charged. Like a bullfighter the young soldier stepped neatly to one side as almost a ton of angry bull thundered by. He was later to say that the discipline of army

219

life was partly what saved him because he remained cool and completely calm thinking only of the best way, technically, to achieve his desired end.

When the bull had completed its first charge it turned to face the young soldier again. This time it was about sixty yards away when it began its charge. The soldier said that he fired several times and each time the bullet was perfectly placed yet it had no more effect on the bison than a pea from a peashooter.

What followed was extraordinary: the bull charged at least fifteen times. Each time the soldier stood his ground and fired, hitting the bull each time. Each time the bull turned, ran off and gave the soldier time to reload before charging again. At the fifteenth charge the bull bore down on the soldier at a terrific speed before dropping stone dead about twenty feet before it reached him. No examination of the bison gave any clue as to its extraordinary behaviour.

THE BRILLIANCE OF THE IRISH

WEXFORD, IRELAND, 1911

Poachers have always been a feature of the shooting world. Centuries ago a man could be hanged for taking a pheasant and the rights of property were such that keepers were perfectly entitled to shoot a poacher on sight or to set mantraps that would take a man's leg off and guarantee him a lingering death from gangrene. Then the pendulum began to swing the other way until by the twentieth century the poacher had a reputation as a lovable rogue who was probably just poaching to save his family from starvation. If caught he would probably be fined a few shillings or let off with a caution. Until relatively recently poachers took birds mainly for their own consumption, but as people travelled greater distances by car and traditional industries vanished leaving large numbers of people unemployed, so poaching became a far more brutal business – today it's virtually an industry in itself in some areas with hundreds of birds slaughtered in a night.

As poaching became a systematic and lucrative activity among criminal gangs so the old poachers vanished – along with the extraordinary wiliness for which they were famous.

They were also famous for their cheek and their wit. One famous Irish poacher was known for his extraordinary ability to escape detection. He was a champion runner and if challenged would always bolt and could never then be caught. He was also an excellent shot and on more than one occasion

he cheekily offered to give the local gentry – English of course
– shooting lessons.

Eventually he'd been seen so many times near the local
shoot's pens that he was taken up by the police anyway and
charged with trespassing with intent. He denied it, of course,
and there was little hard evidence against him, but he was
taken before the local magistrate who admonished him and
declared that he would send him to prison.

The magistrate called a witness for the prosecution who was
actually a friend of the poacher, but also a man whose
brilliance and slipperiness in argument was legendary.

After the accusation that the poacher had fired at a certain
place on a certain day the magistrate asked the witness: 'Did
you see the shot fired?'

'No, I only heard it,' came the reply.

'Then your evidence is not satisfactory. You may stand
down,' said the magistrate.

The witness turned his back on the judge and started to
walk down the steps out of the witness box laughing loudly.
Outraged by this total lack of respect for the court the
magistrate made the witness return to the stand.

'How dare you laugh in court?' asked the magistrate. 'Do
you realise it is tantamount to contempt of court, a serious
offence?'

'Did you see me laugh, your honour?' asked the witness.

'No sir, but I heard you,' was the angry reply.

'Then your evidence is not satisfactory, you may stand
down,' said the witness with a grin.

The packed court dissolved in howls of laughter.

ARCHDUKE'S NARROW ESCAPE

WILTSHIRE, 1913

The Great War was sparked off by the assassination of Archduke Franz Ferdinand of Austria, but history might have been very different if the archduke had not had a narrow escape on the English shooting field just a year earlier when he'd been a guest of the Duke of Portland.

The sixth Duke of Portland was a keen shot – like virtually every landowner in Edwardian Britain, but he was also well connected right across Europe and frequently had foreign heads of state to stay. He tended to mix these with a liberal sprinkling of kings and princes and it was not uncommon to find that the guests at a Portland shooting day some crisp November consisted (as it did on one well-documented occasion) of King Carlos of Portugal, the King of Spain and Archduke Franz Ferdinand of Austria among others. Portland always ranked his guests in order of shooting ability (whether or not they were good company was quite irrelevant) and Franz Ferdinand apparently always took pride of place as a marksman, with Portugal second and Spain third. It took the archduke just a few days to get used to the high flying pheasants so loved of the English aristocracy (Ferdinand was actually an expert rifleman) and after their first week together Portland pronounced him 'certainly the equal of most of my friends'.

Then in December 1913 the archduke found himself shooting, along with a mixed bag of European guests, on a day of deep snow. The archduke was shooting with two loaders, one of whom slipped and fell. The gun the man was carrying went off as it hit the ground and both barrels were discharged, the shot passing within a foot of the archduke's head.

For years afterwards the Duke of Portland would say to anyone who would listen, 'I have often wondered if the Great War might not have been averted or at least postponed had the archduke met his death then and not at Sarajevo in the following year.'

BIGGEST OF ALL

BUCKINGHAMSHIRE, 1913

The biggest bag of game ever shot in one day in Great Britain was probably at Hall Barn, Beaconsfield, Buckinghamshire on the Burtley Beat. Here on 18 December 1913 seven guns – George V, the Prince of Wales, Lord Charles Fitzmaurice, Lord Ilchester, Lord Dalhousie, Lord Herbert Vane-Tempest and the Hon H. Stonor – shot 3,937 pheasants, 3 partridges, 4 rabbits and 1 various (probably a pigeon) making a total of 3,945.

This bag (outrageous by modern standards) eclipsed, at least in terms of pheasants, the bag made at Water Priory, Yorkshire on the Golden Valley Beat on 5 December 1909 when eight guns – the Duke of Roxburghe, Lord Dalhousie, Lord Lovat, Lord Savile, Lord Londesborough, Lord Cecil Manners, Lord Chelsea and the Hon C.H.W. Wilson – shot 3,824 pheasants, 15 partridges, 526 hares, 92 rabbits and 3 various, making a total of 4,460. The following day the same guns had already shot more than 3,000 pheasants by lunchtime when they stopped shooting because of the very high winds.

But the most outrageous day's shooting of all occurred on Count Louis Karolyi's estate at Totmeyer, Hungary when 6,125 pheasants were shot in one day together with 150 hares and 50 partridges.

At Blenheim Palace in Oxfordshire on 7 October 1898 6,943 rabbits were bagged by just five guns on seven drives, but this was at a time when myxomatosis had yet to reach these shores and for

225

every rabbit that ended up in the pot another two continued to bounce across the meadows. And of course the bag was easier to achieve in days when there were so many estate servants that they could get up early and block all the entrances to the rabbit warrens while the rabbits were still out nibbling the grass. When the rabbit drives began the poor old rabbits had no choice but to run, for they could no longer get back underground.

Away from these aristocratic shoots, on 26 October 1826 at Whittlesea Mere in Cambridgeshire at precisely 5 a.m. Colonel Hawker (he was a stickler for keeping precise records) downed 504 starlings with one shot from his massive punt gun – the huge double gun contained nearly two pounds of fine shot. It took two days to pick up all the tiny birds. Hawker was alleged to have killed something like 3,000,000 head of game in his lifetime – a figure that seems to have grown with his reputation in shooting circles – but a careful look at his published books reveal that figure to be closer to 18,000.

Lord Malmesbury in forty seasons, which ended in 1840, calculated that he had walked 36,200 miles or very nearly one and a half times round the world in pursuit of a total bag of 38,934. To achieve that bag he had fired 54,987 shots. Perhaps more remarkable than these figures is the fact that Amesbury bothered to keep such precise records.

These are well attested big days. When we reach the legendary days for which there is only tentative evidence the record day has to be that recorded by the Reverend William Daniel. He says that in October 1797 Prince Liechtenstein and eleven other guns shooting in Germany managed to bag (in just one day) a little over 39,000 partridges and hares.

In England it is clear that between the beginning of the Victorian era and the end of the Edwardian period game shooting had gone from a small-scale operation to big business. The total amount of game shot each year increased fifteenfold. Game books showing these huge bags would once have been displayed proudly in the halls of great houses, but as taxes began to eat into the lavish lifestyles of the great, shooting became a quieter affair.

And then it was all over. After the Great War this kind of excess quite rightly seemed unjustifiable, and as many of the low paid rural workers who had made the massive rearing operation on which big days relied had been killed, it was a practical impossibility too.

HIGH VELOCITY

ENGLAND, 1914

One of the biggest problems for the British royal family and the aristocracy generally during the First World War was the fact that so many of their relatives and friends were German. It is common knowledge that the British royal family changed its name from Saxe-Coburg to Windsor after the start of hostilities, but many other English aristocrats found they suddenly had to cut their ties with half their families and many of their friends.

For the Kaiser the war must have been similarly inconvenient as he had been accustomed for many years to visiting his friends and relatives in England to shoot their grouse and pheasants – the English tradition of shooting was one he loved dearly.

He was said to be a charming man, decent, generous and generally well behaved, but the same could not be said for those of his friends who travelled to England with him.

At several shoots it was discovered that one or other of his friends, bored with standing in line waiting for the birds to come over them, gave up their shotguns and used rifles instead. If they saw pheasants in the trees or on the ground they would shoot at them even if the beaters were close behind.

On one occasion a baron who had accompanied the German emperor to England just a few months before war was declared spent the day at a pheasant drive trying to shoot the birds in flight – with a rifle! High-velocity bullets whizzed everywhere, much to the terror of the other guns. The problem of inviting the Kaiser and his friend to further shoots was solved because once the war began it was no longer possible anyway.

PHEASANTS THEN SHELLS

FRANCE, 1915

All across the western front between 1914 and 1917 pheasants and partridges flourished where soldiers from Britain, France and Germany died in their tens of thousands. Soldiers reported seeing pheasants and partridges carrying on with their lives completely unconcerned as 5.9s and 18-pound shells burst all around them. When they weren't perched on a broken stump of a tree in the middle of no-man's-land they could be found grazing gently across the shell-pocked ground, and close up against the firing line soldiers frequently disturbed hares on their forms. Bizarre though the whole thing sounds, it actually made sense from the animals' point of view. The closer the animals were to the front, the better the feeding, because the ground was constantly being churned and turned by explosives throwing up good things to eat.

One January night in 1915 a young officer wandered into a dugout with which he was unfamiliar and there quite by chance met a man he'd known at home in Ireland. The two men had shot together at home so they decided to try for a few pheasants the following day as they were not, temporarily, in the front-line trenches but some way back from them. The two were able to muster two 28-bore walking-stick shotguns and they took with them one of the men's batmen who carried a service rifle and two sandbags.

It was misty the next day when they set off – perfect conditions given that the whole thing would have been impossible on a clear day as the Germans would have been able to see them and they'd have been quickly shot by snipers.

They reached a field a little behind the front-line trenches where they had seen birds feeding. The field still had tobacco plants growing in it from earlier peacetime days and the only difficulty was the large number of unexploded German shells which littered the ground. As they walked across the field they put up several pheasants, a few partridges and snipe. They bagged a few and then noticed that the Germans had clearly heard the shots and assumed there was a battery in the area, for seconds later the air was filled with the sound of screaming shells heading towards the two sportsmen and their beater. They decided to beat a hasty retreat before they were bagged by the Germans.

PHEASANTS IN THE TRENCHES

FRANCE, 1916

It's a little known fact that throughout the First World War, all along the line of the trenches in Normandy and Flanders, the British obsession with sport – that is shooting, fishing and hunting – continued unabated. There was of course a class division – it was the officers who set out after the rabbits and hares and partridges that had flourished during the years in which men had killed each other rather than them. And as rations were short for the British, and boring when they were not short, the chance of a roasted hare or partridge was irresistible.

But of course a day's rabbit or partridge shooting had to be carefully organised in an environment where bullets and shells from the German trenches were never far away. Lieutenant Galwey Foley described a day in 1916 when he heard a few pheasants crowing somewhere behind the front-line trenches. He decided to have a go for them, but knowing that German snipers were eternally vigilant as well as being equipped with highly sophisticated telescopic sights, he decided that a careful strategy was essential if he were to bag the birds without himself being shot by the Germans. Galwey Foley had hunted pheasants and other birds in and around the trenches many times before so he knew the ropes – the trick was to stalk your birds by dashing from shell hole to shell hole. This sounds more dangerous than it perhaps was. The Germans would always be watching but each dash between shell holes – just so long as it was a dash – would not give the German sniper, however good he was, the chance to get a mark on the pheasant hunter.

So Galwey Foley set off at a crouching dash in pursuit of his pheasants. He tripped and fell a couple of times but no shots rang out from the other side. Soon within sight of the pheasants, he took careful aim and bagged one with his rifle before stuffing it inside his coat and crawling back to his trench for breakfast.

Partridges were particularly plentiful over the trenches but very difficult to hit with the single bullet from a rifle. In letters home Galwey Foley complained again and again that he was sorely in need of a shotgun for these birds, but it is doubtful if the army would have looked kindly on a request for a 12-bore.

Galwey Foley was particularly intrigued by a party of about fourteen partridges that flew over the same part of the British lines every morning before settling among the corpses and mud of no-man's-land for the rest of the day. The party would then flight back over British lines in the evening presumably to feed on some abandoned field of wheat somewhere in the rear.

One morning, just before 'stand down', Galwey Foley heard the unmistakable honk of a skein of geese coming from behind the British trenches. The birds soon appeared heading towards the German lines. Galwey Foley shouted at the men on the British firing step to give the birds rapid fire in the hope of bringing one down. This was done but the birds passed unscathed. As they reached the German trenches the birds were greeted by a similar fusillade, but with the same result.

On the morning that Galwey Foley heard the geese he saw a pigeon alight on a blackened stump of a tree some sixty yards to the rear of the German lines. Immediately there was a massive fusillade from the German gunners – it was so loud that many British soldiers thought that an attack had begun. In fact, the Germans – at least a couple of dozen of them – were determined to get that pigeon. And not just for the fun of it – rations were as short for the Germans as for the British and they wanted to eat that bird. In fact they did hit the bird and all that day and into the next night the British kept a sniper with his rifle trained on and near the dead bird hoping that a German, eager for a little pigeon pie, would try to retrieve it. One man did leap up out of the German trenches, but after a few bullets whipped up the ground around his feet he dived for cover and that was the end of that.

Mornings in the trenches for Galwey Foley were devoted to shooting rats with his revolver, for the rats, which had never had so much food – they ate the bodies of the dead – were as big as cats. One memorable day Galwey Foley saw an army cat turn a corner in the trench and come face to face with a huge rat. The two animals stared at each other for a few seconds and then the cat fled.

THE END OF AN
EXTRAORDINARY LIFE

AFRICA, 1917

Frederick Courtenay Selous was born in 1851 and died in 1917. From the age of six he was an obsessive hunter, shooter, butterfly and bird collector. He lived at a time when Europe and Africa seemed to have an inexhaustible supply of game and Selous was determined from the start to shoot and stuff as much of it as possible.

At his first school he lay on the hard floorboards with just a blanket so he would get used to the hardships of the hunting field. He was continually at war with the masters at Rugby School because he was never there. When he should have been at lessons he was out collecting eggs and butterflies or shooting duck, geese, gulls – anything and everything he could. He once travelled fifteen miles late in the evening to a famous heronry where he stripped off, swam across a freezing lake, climbed a sixty foot tree and helped himself to two eggs. He was back in school by morning, but the eggs were confiscated until the masters learned of his efforts to get them. They were so impressed they returned the eggs to him.

On another occasion, while shooting with a number of aristocrats in Germany, he was about to lose a duck he'd shot that had fallen into the swiftly flowing Rhine. His fellow shots looked on in astonishment as he stripped off and dived into the river, swimming around ice floes to retrieve his bird.

His parents sent Selous to Africa where his most extraordinary days' shooting were to take place. In one day he shot

22 elephants and collected 700 pounds of ivory from them. Now such destruction seems indefensible, but in Selous's day it would never have occurred to anyone that African game might one day be threatened with extinction.

On sighting an elephant Selous would instantly remove his trousers as he found it easier to pursue them in his underpants, and as his London rifle was stolen when he arrived in Africa he simply bought a local 4-bore and used that instead. It was apparently a terrible gun that kicked violently and was in constant danger of exploding. It was also almost impossible to lift, weighing in at nearly 20 pounds.

Selous may have felt a slight pang about the amount of game he shot in Africa, for in the books he later wrote he paints endlessly vivid pictures of the sheer abundance of African game in his day.

Whether out shooting or not Selous's diet consisted almost entirely of moose fat and very strong tea. He found that this combination gave him strength and courage. At camp his tea was left boiling and stewing all day and it was the evening cup he loved best.

Once, staying in a London hotel, he tested his rifle by firing at a chimney stack on the other side of the street. As he left the hotel he confided to several people in the crowd of alarmed neighbours that the sound appeared to come from the rooms above.

When he died Selous had collected thousands of birds and butterflies from all over Europe and Africa. He'd shot dozens of examples of every big-game animal in the world, but when retirement loomed at the age of 63 in 1914 he volunteered for military service. While leading his company against a force of Germans four times their size in East Africa, he was killed at the age of 65.

A REMARKABLE ESCAPE

CEYLON, 1918

The assistant government agent at Trincomalee in what is now Sri Lanka, was a Mr G.S. Wodehouse. The agent for the Eastern Province was a Mr Festing. The two men were acquaintances, even friends. On 18 August they decided to walk the first part of a tour they often made through the villages of Madawachi towards Kaddukulum. Part of the reason for this tour was to inspect a tank. Festing walked ahead along the narrow sandy road that was bounded on both sides by dense jungle. He carried a double-barrelled shotgun loaded with No 8 shot (which is small) on the off chance that they would encounter a jungle cock for breakfast. Wodehouse walked just behind his friend carrying a stout walking stick. Half a dozen local villagers and headmen followed behind.

Just before 8 a.m., when the men were still about two miles from their destination, Festing, by now about twenty feet ahead of Wodehouse, turned where the path made a sharp right turn. As soon as he turned the path Wodehouse saw Festing go rigid and then in a second he had put the gun up to his shoulder. Immediately, as if they sensed what was about to happen, all the headmen and villagers walking behind Wodehouse vanished off the path and into the jungle, scattering in all directions.

As the villagers vanished Wodehouse reached the turn and saw directly ahead of him two bears, side by side, charging down towards Festing as fast as they could go. They had only been ten yards away when they'd seen Festing so they were almost on top of him within seconds and they were so close that their roars were deafening.

Festing said later that the two bears had been standing on their hind legs when he'd first seen them. They'd been sniffing vigorously, probably trying to work out where the humans were so they could avoid them. Had they been facing away from Festing as he turned the corner they would almost certainly have bolted in the other direction and away from him, but at thirty feet a face-to-face confrontation with a bear looks to the bear like imminent attack.

Festing quickly fired both barrels and one bear ran off to the side of the path and into the jungle. The other continued its charge, running straight at Festing and knocking him down. The bear then leaped on to Festing and the two rolled around together on the ground, Festing swearing at the top of his voice and thrashing his arms and legs, the bear roaring continually. Wodehouse ran over to the two and seizing the gun, which had fallen on the ground, he began belting the bear round the head with it until the stock broke. He couldn't reload and fire as all the cartridges were in Festing's pocket.

By now the bear had weakened, but realising its new attacker was still on his feet, the bear left Festing on the ground, got up on its hind legs and chased after Wodehouse, who couldn't get out of the way in time. The bear got Wodehouse's arm into his mouth and the two fell against a bank, the bear all the while kicking out at Wodehouse and leaving deep scratches on its legs. Had the bear not been weakened by all the blows around its head from the gun there is no doubt that Wodehouse's injuries would have been much worse – in fact a bear in possession of all its faculties would have stripped his leg to the bone in seconds.

Even in its weakened state the bear was crushing Wodehouse's arm badly, but just when he was about to pass out, Festing, all bloodied and half blinded though he was, picked himself up, came up behind the bear with the gun barrels and started belting it across the head again until it released Wodehouse. As soon as it did so the two men ran for their lives and when, fifty yards away, they glanced back they saw that the bear too had had enough and had vanished into the jungle.

As suddenly as they'd vanished the headmen and villagers reappeared. One, who carried a big machete, said he had run very fast into the jungle to cut sticks with which to kill the bear. Wodehouse commented wryly that he could certainly vouch for the bit about running fast.

When they took stock of the situation the two men found they were really quite badly injured. Wodehouse's arm had been bitten through to the bone by the bear's large incisors. Festing's thigh had been badly lacerated in several places and his face was a mass of cuts and bruises. They patched each other up as best they could and travelled fifteen miles in a bullock cart to the nearest field hospital. On the way they saw a jungle cock, but all thought of breakfast had long vanished.

The bears were almost certainly a mother and cub. The cub was the one that had run into the bush as soon as the first shot was fired, but the mother, with the instinct to protect her offspring, had faced the full charge of the gun.

INDESTRUCTIBLE STAG

SCOTLAND, 1920

The writer J.F. Wharton was staying in the remote hills of West Sutherland. There was little water in the river so he could not try for salmon, so instead he decided to see if he could get any stalking. His luck was in and together with another sportsman who was staying at the same hotel he went off one September morning with the estate stalker. On their climb the old stalker explained that an old well-known stag that had been seen and stalked for many years had returned to the hills round about. The stalker said that the old stag needed to be taken out and so the party agreed to try for it.

As they climbed ever higher the old stalker told Wharton about the stag. He was, it seemed, at least twenty years old, which was remarkable in itself given the harsh conditions of the open hill. He was known over a very wide area and to a great many stalkers, many of whom had tried to shoot him without success. Age had made him remarkably good at sensing danger and it was difficult to pin him down as he wandered unusually far over the hills crossing many different estates. The old stalker explained that now, in September, he came to this ground but always with a young stag who the men called his toady – basically the young stag was there to give the old stag an extra pair of eyes whenever danger threatened.

'This ground,' the stalker continued, 'is very difficult when it comes to stalking. When you think you've reached a vantage point from which to check the position of a deer there will always be hidden ground somewhere between you and the deer, ground that may help give your presence away. Every gully and crevice might contain an animal that will bolt, spoiling everything.'

The day wore on and when they stopped for lunch Wharton took his spyglass and checked an area of rock about a mile distant and just above a small group of hinds. The stalker checked the same area and then hissed, 'Do ye see him? The old stag. He's there with his toady just behind him.'

Wharton could just make the old stag out and said so.

'I've tried for him more than a dozen times now with no success,' continued the old stalker. 'And every stalker on every estate round about has tried for him. Only one ever even got a shot at him. We think he was hit as there was a small trail of blood, but he vanished and returned a year later as healthy as ever. He leads a charmed life.'

Moving carefully round rocks and across crevices the men moved towards the old stag. It took over an hour to cover half the distance keeping downwind of the deer, but when they checked again through their monoculars (stalkers never use binoculars) he was still there.

'It's him all right,' said the old stalker. Wharton could see him more clearly now, with his yellowish coat and his head curled round his flank as he slept. And all the while the younger stag – the toady as the old stalker called him – kept a wary eye on the surrounding countryside.

The men knew that to keep downwind of him and get close enough for a shot they would have to take a wide circle round him and get to a spur of rock well above his position. By mid-afternoon they were inching their way into position, lying flat and slithering on their bellies.

With just a hundred yards or so to go they took another careful look to check his position and the old man sighed.

'He's done it again,' he said and sure enough Wharton could see the toady moving out of sight and the old stag with him.

Next morning it was another man's turn to try for the stag and Wharton stayed at the hotel, but he agreed to drive that afternoon to a landmark bridge where he would meet the others at the end of their day on the hill. Snoozing by the roadside that afternoon Wharton was barely aware of time passing until something made him look up. And there in full view and moving across the ground they'd covered the previous day was the old stag with his young lookout.

Wharton expected from that moment on to hear a shot, but nothing happened and when the old stalker and his companion arrived Wharton assumed that the remarkable old stag must once again have done his Houdini act and escaped. But then the old stalker asked for the rope and said they would need all three of them to bring the stag down.

Wharton had had a bet with the other young man about who would get the stag and, assuming he simply hadn't heard the shot, asked how much he owed his companion. 'Nothing,' came the reply.

Then the old stalker explained what had happened. The stag and his toady had indeed been too smart for the stalker, but after moving around and trying to come at him from a number of different angles they came face to face completely by accident high up on the edge of a steep ravine. They were just twenty yards from each other but the rifle was in its case. Wheeling about, the old stag crashed into the younger animal, lost its footing and fell into the deep ravine. It was killed instantly. The old stalker remarked ruefully on the irony of the stag's death – the young animal that had saved its life so often had ultimately been responsible for its death.

MAN ON A WHITE HORSE

TIERRA DEL FUEGO, 1920

Tierra del Fuego, that remote, almost forgotten area at the tip of South America, was once reasonably densely populated by local Indians. Then, in the 1860s and 1870s Spanish settlers moved into the area in greater numbers and their sheep and cattle encouraged the Indians to become poachers. This in turn led to the government declaring that it would pay a dollar for each Indian killed. They were simply a nuisance and the Spaniards in charge didn't really classify them as human. Thousands of Indians were shot over the next few years until the bounty was lifted. By then the remaining Indians had left the area anyway. The reputation of Tierra del Fuego as a vast, ghostly and uninhabited region grew from this time. Very few Europeans knew anything of Tierra del Fuego until well after the Second World War, so it is not surprising that accounts of the region published by an Englishman in 1922 aroused a fair amount of interest. The author, clearly a military man, never revealed his identity and although his book is now completely forgotten it contains some fascinating descriptions of the region. The Englishman wrote under the pseudonym Banderas and his book, *Shooting in South America*, is in part at least a guide to South American game shooting.

One autumn morning in 1920 Banderas and his team of beaters and bag carriers decided on a duck-shooting trip to a vast lagoon. Those doing the shooting lined out along a causeway while dogs and men coming from either end of the lagoon drove the duck towards them. All the men, beaters and shooters included, knew of the existence of a strange man who always turned up at shoots like this. He rode a white horse, was unkempt and savage looking and no one had the least idea where he lived.

No sooner had the guns lined out along the causeway on the day in question than Caballo Blanco appeared on the horizon like a villain in a cowboy film. He moved along the edge of the lagoon and through the shallows helping push the birds along.

Banderas later heard what little was known of this strange man. He never spoke or washed or got down off his horse. He lived, it appeared, in the mountains and scavenged his food – he had been seen eating the rotting carcasses of sheep, cats, foxes and even skunks. When one of his horses died he camped by it until he'd eaten it all. At the end of the lagoon shoot he was given a few duck to take away with him and Banderas's beaters assured him that Caballo Blanco would soon be eating the ducks raw.

PSYCHING THE LION

AFRICA, 1920

Stewart Edward White hunted in Africa in the early years of the twentieth century. He was a rich American with a passion for trophy hunting. He wanted to bag at least one each of all the big species – lions, tigers, leopards, black rhino, white rhino and elephants – and he travelled the world to do it. He was nearly killed on several occasions, but was the first to admit that the most extraordinary thing he'd ever seen while out shooting was an unarmed African villager who stumbled by accident across a very angry lion.

The villager had agreed to take White out to look for smaller game – various species of deer, birds and even monkeys – and they had travelled only a few miles along a well-worn path from the village when, sixty feet ahead of White, the villager stopped in his tracks. He didn't signal to White, but from the sudden way the man had stopped and his absolute rigidity, the American knew instantly that he had seem something very dangerous indeed. Hoping to get a shot at whatever it was, the American worked his way slowly around the African, keeping as low as possible and under or behind what little cover there was.

After a few moments he had manoeuvred himself into a position where he could at least see what had apparently turned the African to stone. What he saw was a huge male lion sitting on its haunches and staring directly at the guide, who was about sixty feet away.

The standoff was extraordinary. Neither man nor animal

moved a muscle and it seemed to make no difference that, in theory at least, the lion must have sensed that another man was lurking nearby.

Time seemed to stand still and then the African did something that made the American think he must be dreaming. He leaned forward until his downward stretching hands were about a foot from the ground, while tilting his head back in order to maintain eye contact with the lion. He then began a sort of crouching shuffle towards the lion. White probably should have tried a shot at the animal since it was sitting absolutely still, but he was afraid that if he missed, the lion would charge the African and probably kill him before White could get off another shot. If the truth were known he was probably also fascinated by the extraordinary ritual the African seemed to be performing.

When the shuffling man had reduced the distance between him and the lion by about half, the animal, which until then had maintained an absolute stillness, began to swish its tail. It then broke off eye contact and looked for some time to one side, almost as if it was afraid to meet the unrelenting gaze of the African. Twenty paces were left between the man and the lion when, in the time it takes to blink, the lion turned on its heel and fled.

White talked for a long time to the African who maintained that in his village all the men, women and children knew that if they encountered a lion the trick he had just performed was their only real chance of surviving the encounter. The man would not be drawn on whether or not it was always successful.

In nineteenth-century Africa firearms were almost unheard of outside the hands of Europeans. Native people had to rely on spears or they simply did their best to avoid areas that they knew were frequented by large dangerous animals. If the worst came to the worst they used special tricks, like staring out a lion, as a last resort and based on generations of experience they obviously worked at least some of the time. There are numerous reports of unarmed Africans escaping what would normally have been certain death, but few of these are stranger than the tale of one of White's bearers who was caught off-guard by an angry buffalo. The animal had clearly already been attacked when the bearer stumbled across it, and of course the buffalo was in no position to distinguish between this harmless human and one, now long gone, who fired an annoying arrow which was still stuck in its flank. No sooner had the buffalo spotted the young man than it charged and he being unarmed simply ran for it.

A buffalo in a rage is a very swift animal and the bearer must have known that in seconds it would catch him and trample him to death. There were no trees to climb so the bearer, with great presence of mind, threw himself into a shallow depression that was half concealed by a rock. The buffalo stopped dead at the depression and tried to get the man with his horns, but it could only do this by putting its head down and then rooting carefully about in the narrow gap where the man lay. As soon as the buffalo's nose was within reach the bearer grabbed it and gave it a fearful wrench. The buffalo's nose is extremely sensitive and with a bellow of pain it lifted its head and ran as fast as it could from what it probably thought was a huge and very angry bee. The bearer was delighted with his victory and it was the talk of the village for months afterwards.

BIRD STRIKE

DEVON, 1922

A fully grown pheasant is a heavy bird and, although they are reluctant flyers, once they get going pheasants are capable of great speeds – which is why it is as well to watch out when lots of them are about.

At a shoot in a remote part of north Devon in the 1920s, a group of farmers who'd been neighbours and friends for years discovered just how much damage a falling pheasant can do while they were walking through a remote strip of woodland at the top of a hill.

As they tramped along a pheasant got up ahead of them, but instead of flying directly away from them it took off almost vertically and then turned back to fly over their heads, at which point one of the farmers decided to shoot at it.

They watched as the bird somersaulted and began to fall – directly towards them. They stood astonished looking up and wondering where it would fall and it was almost in slow motion that they saw it plunge on to the head of one of their number. The man stood rigid for a moment, then his legs crumpled and he fell senseless to the ground. The other guns surrounded him and tried to revive him, but without success. One of them ran to a house and set off by horse to the nearest village where there was a doctor.

It turned out that the pheasant, clearly seeking its revenge for being shot at, had fractured the man's skull. He was to spend the next two weeks in hospital recovering. For days he had no idea where he was and the doctors feared he might never recover. When he did finally come round he remembered nothing of the incident and in fact could remember nothing that had happened in the previous two months.

No one recorded his reaction when he woke one morning, still in his hospital bed, to find himself surrounded by his shooting friends, one of whom held aloft a present for the injured man – a stuffed pheasant and the very one that had nearly killed him.

ONE UP ON THE LAWYERS

IRELAND, 1922

Poaching in remote parts of Britain was a way of life for the poor right up to the 1950s. In Ireland the abundance of game and the remote chance of detection meant that most poachers would never appear before the magistrate. Occasionally of course a poacher would be caught, where a particularly severe landlord – usually English – made a determined effort to protect his game. This would make the landlord intensely unpopular among the local people, but if it came to court any lawyer foolish enough to take the prosecution brief could look forward to years of ostracism. The eternal dislike of lawyers meant too that the local people were always delighted when someone got one over on a barrister or solicitor. It didn't happen often but when it did it was remembered for many years and the tale would be told and retold throughout the district much to the chagrin of the lawyer in question.

A very fat, English, red-faced lawyer who went round all the petty sessions courts had a reputation as a man who liked to put the country people down. He would talk to them in court as if they were idiots and they resented this hugely, but could do little about it. Then one day the great red-faced lawyer, who weighed twenty stone if he weighed an ounce, was up in court prosecuting a poor local man who'd been caught with a few rabbits in a bag. The poor man was popular locally and had a large family, so there was much support for him, but for some reason the fat lawyer was particularly keen on this occasion to make sure the man was convicted.

The poor man called an old blind woman from his village to give evidence in his defence. He said that he'd called out to her from his little garden that evening and that, as he'd spent the whole evening in his garden working and had spoken to her every now and then, he could not have been out looking for other people's game in the woods round about. The fat-faced lawyer said to the judge: 'My Lord, much as we sympathise with the plight of this poor old blind woman we cannot admit her evidence as she cannot have seen a thing. She did not see the accused in his garden and he may have slipped away to the woods between his occasional remarks to her. And voices over a distance may be mistook.'

On hearing this, the old woman turned her head towards where she knew the judge would be sitting and said: 'Certainly I'm blind and have been since birth, but I never mistake a man's voice. It's like feeling a man's face – it'll always tell me who he is as good as if I could see him plain in front of me.'

'My Lord,' repeated the fat lawyer, 'she is blind. It would not be fair to admit her evidence.'

The judge tended to agree with the old woman, however, and said: 'I think it is fair and just. It is indeed wonderful how the blind can identify people by the feel of their faces.'

The fat lawyer thought he would prove his point by putting his face close to the old woman's and then disguising his voice.

'Now my dear,' said the lawyer in a guttural tone, 'who have we here?'

The old woman replied, 'Now, that voice I do not recognise, but put your face up to me and I will put my hand on it and know you in a second.'

The lawyer pushed his great round face to within a few inches of the old woman's and she put her hand out and touched him. Straight away she turned in the direction of the judge and said: 'It's a terrible thing, your honour, to make fun of a poor old blind woman. This is no face at all I'm feeling. Sure it's a great soft, fat arse!'

The whole court dissolved into shrieks of laughter and the clerk of the court could not restore order for some twenty minutes. The poacher was acquitted and for years afterwards until he left the district the fat lawyer was known everywhere as arseface.

SHOOTING ON SKATES

NORFOLK, 1922

The men who lived and worked on the fens of East Anglia before every inch of that region was turned into a vast prairie, were a strange, independent, not to say eccentric bunch. They lived by shooting wildfowl in winter and by catching fish and eels in summer with a bit of farmwork thrown in for good measure. But it is not generally known that until the 1930s Britain's greatest skaters came from the Fens. The reason was simple. Skating had come to the area probably with the Dutch engineers who began draining the peaty waters in the seventeenth century, but by the end of the nineteenth century the local men and women were masters of the art. Until well into the twentieth century they still used iron blades lashed with leather thongs to the soles of an old pair of boots. In earlier times they'd used animal bones.

East Anglia was ideal for skating because the land flooded every year and as the floods were often shallow and widespread they froze easily, providing numerous skating rinks.

But the skates and the frozen fields provided an enormous advantage for those fenmen not averse to a little poaching. The speed skaters would strap on their boots, sling a gun and a bag over their shoulders and work the edges of woods where the fields were frozen. At the first sign of a keeper or policeman they would be off across the fields on their skates and any pursuer would simply fall head over heels if he attempted to pursue them.

Legend has it that the only time one of the skating poachers got caught was when a crafty policeman got wind of what was going on in one area and lay in wait at the edge of a frozen field where dozens of pheasants had already been spirited away. When dawn came the policeman spotted a figure with a gun speeding silently across the ice. The figure stopped at the edge of the wood and waited. A few moments later he'd fired into the trees at the roosting pheasants. With a brace in his bag he was about to set off for home when he heard the policeman's shout. Not in the least worried he pushed off and built up a bit of speed on the ice, chuckling to himself as he went. But imagine his horror when he glanced back only to see the policeman belting after him and also on skates. The poacher was apprehended and was fined three shillings.

IDENTICAL BEARDS

NORFOLK, 1923

King George V is probably best known today for his distinctive beard, which he wore throughout his adult life. Less well known was the king's sense of humour, which manifested itself in some decidedly eccentric ways.

When he shot at Sandringham he insisted that one of the estate workers should load for him despite the fact that, as a rule, it was always better to shoot using a loader you knew really well. Familiarity lessened the chances of the guns being passed awkwardly or at the wrong time.

But the king, being the king, made his decision and that was that.

It took the king's friends some time to realise that the reason he liked this particular loader was that the man could have been his twin. The estate worker was the same height and build and – best of all – he had a beard the very mirror image of the king's.

Some courtiers no doubt felt that the man should shave or grow his beard in such a way that the similarity was lessened, but the king would have none of it. To this day no one really knows if it was coincidence or the king's decision, but having shot together several times the king and his loader began gradually to wear the same clothes. At first it was just that their coats were similar, then their breeches and shoes and stockings. The identical clothing, combined with the remarkable similarity of the two men's beards, their identical build and demeanour, was highly unsettling, although no one dared say so.

Close friends of the king let on that he was delighted at the confusion and embarrassment constantly caused by his apparent doppelgänger – every time he went shooting at Sandringham, he noticed that neither his guests nor the beaters or household servants was ever quite sure who was addressing whom. The loader seemed to enjoy the fun too, particularly when, on one occasion, an earl spoke to him in such deferential terms that the king, who was standing nearby, had to walk quickly away and stifle howls of laughter.

SHOOTING ASLEEP AND AWAKE

YORKSHIRE, 1927

Shooting was once considered far too brutal for the gentler sex, although there are examples of women who became as enthusiastic about the sport as any man. The dangers of shooting were many and they affected women and men whether they shot or not. Beaters were often peppered with shot by overenthusiastic sportsmen, loaders, who had to stand right behind their masters in the shooting field, might be hit by a stray pellet or even knocked out by a fat pheasant falling like a stone out of the sky. The same risk was run by wives out to watch their partners in the butts. But at least one woman suffered injury from a shooting man in a much more unusual way.

Mrs David Stanhope had accompanied her husband to Yorkshire for a week's grouse shooting. He was an experienced shot but fanatical and after a bad opening day his personality changed. At night he appeared to relive his terrible day in the field. He thrashed about shouting 'Bird over!' at the top of his voice, or bellowed 'God damn this gun' as if he was really about to take a shot and his Purdey had jammed.

The first night of these dreams lasted, so his wife later confessed, about an hour. She was not in the least concerned, thinking it was just the excitement engendered by the first day's shooting after long months of no shooting at all.

But on the second night the shouting and thrashing about were worse and she had great difficulty waking him. 'Mark over!' he shouted at the top of his voice and then 'Leg down bird!'

He did eventually wake and he apologised when she told him what he'd been doing but he claimed to have no memory of anything.

As soon as he fell asleep again the ranting and rolling resumed. On the third night the situation had got so bad that during one particularly forceful encounter with a ghostly bird – which he'd clearly missed in his dream – he thumped his fist so hard on the pillow (unfortunately not, in fact, his pillow) that he broke his wife's nose and blacked her eye.

Not willing further to risk life and limb, Mrs Stanhope returned to London on the morning train, leaving her husband to thrash about alone on his nightly forays.

HUMOURING THE RICH

YORKSHIRE, 1928

Shooting people could be awful in the days when servants –
even gillies and keepers – were barely considered human by
those who paid their wages. The Duke of Norfolk once told a
cousin who'd objected to having a family argument on the
grounds that the butler and a maid were in the room: 'But they
are servants; as far as we are concerned they do not exist.'

In a milder form, earls and lords, though often more wary
of being too dismissive of gillies and keepers, could be
absurdly condescending to them. Gillies and keepers, however,
were famous for getting their own back, unlike the poor old
domestic servant.

One Scottish keeper would go to great lengths to please a
shooting man he liked, but if he thought he was being badly
treated he would bide his time and get his revenge in a way that
was obvious to all and yet was not so obvious that he could be
sacked for it.

Out on the moors in the late 1920s he spent a long time
looking for a pheasant that the earl of somewhere or other had
shot. The keeper knew that the bird had almost certainly not
been hit at all, but he kept looking anyway. Eventually the
shoot owner approached the old keeper and asked why he was
looking for a bird that several guns had seen escape unscathed.

'Yon man said the bird was doon and I didnae want to
offend him,' said the keeper.

On the same day he had watched an overenthusiastic

shooter trying for grouse at such close quarters that the birds would be fit for nothing at the end of the day. It all got too much when the keeper picked up one bird and found it had a big hole right through it.

'When you can shoot like that, sir,' said the keeper, 'do you not think it would be better to give them law, I mean to shoot them only when they are a little further away?'

On another occasion the old keeper took a very different tack with an equally distinguished shooting guest who treated him in an offhand manner. The guest had complained about everything and always aimed his complaints at the old keeper rather than the beaters or flagmen or even his own loaders. Again and again the old keeper simply put up with reprimands and shouts of irritation, but those who knew him well knew also that this could not last and that he would get his own back.

At last the shooting guest said to the old keeper, 'I found a hair in my gun this morning. See that it does not happen again.'

'Certainly, sir,' came the reply. 'I will see to it. Anything to please ye sir, even fighting if ye like.'

The rebuke caused a few chuckles among the other guns, but it was so subtle that if the distinguished shooter had made a fuss he would have been made to look even more foolish.

MESMERISED ELEPHANT

CEYLON, 1928

Two elephants were proclaimed rogues in Ceylon (now Sri Lanka) in the late 1920s. One had caused trouble by taking a savage dislike to people – if it saw someone it instantly chased them. The other disliked people, domestic animals and cultivated fields. An Englishmen and his friend were given licenses to shoot the two animals and duly set off one November morning in their battered old car. Both men were armed with .400 rifles and plenty of ammunition. They decided to try first for the chocolate-coloured animal whose whereabouts they could apparently discover from the local policeman. Having driven as far as they could through the jungle the two men left their car and travelled the last four miles to the village on foot. When they arrived at the village they settled down for a rest and a smoke while dozens of villagers were sent out to scout for signs of the elephant.

Two hours later a scout returned, having located the animal's track, and the hunters set off into the jungle. After several hours they heard the sound of trumpeting some distance ahead. But there were two elephants and they were only fifty yards ahead.

One of the two hunters moved carefully forward with a tracker until they were within fifteen yards of the elephant, but it was in such deep cover that the hunter was reluctant to shoot. At that range a bungled shot would mean the elephant would charge. As quietly as possible the hunter and his tracker stalked the moving elephant glimpsing it every now and then but never clearly enough for a shot. Then at last the elephant stopped in a tiny clearing. Half an hour later it had still not moved. A slight shift of position gave the hunter the glimpse he'd been waiting for and he fired. It was a bungled shot and with a scream the elephant turned and hurled itself at the hunter and his companion. Running and turning at the same time the hunter fired again but the elephant's blood was up and nothing now it seemed could stop it. The hunter stopped and threw open the breech of his gun, but all the while knowing there would not be time to reload before the elephant killed him.

Then an extraordinary thing happened. The tracker who had been behind the hunter at first was now running a little in front of him and just to one side. In the instant that the hunter glanced across he saw the tracker stop and turn to face the charging elephant as if spellbound; it was as if he was simply waiting for the elephant to run him down and kill him. Then, with the elephant just a few yards away, the tracker suddenly began waving his arms and shouting directly at the elephant.

The elephant stopped in its tracks, throwing up clouds of dust from its massive feet, and gazed at the tracker for what seemed an eternity. It then turned on its heel, bolted and was never seen again despite several hours searching by the hunter and his trackers.

The hunter discovered later that the people of Ceylon believe implicitly in their ability to stop a charging elephant using a series of magical words – in other words a charm. Few Europeans were ever lucky enough to witness the successful use of this charm, but it clearly worked some of the time. However, there were many recorded instances of elephant charmers trying to stop charging elephants and failing – at the cost of their lives. A Vishnu priest who tried to save a party of Europeans, who'd accidentally stumbled across an elephant, using the so-called charm was trampled to death in an instant.

DIVEBOMBER

YORKSHIRE, 1930

On a blustery day on the Yorkshire moors in 1930, a party of six guns were having a very good day grouse shooting. The birds were flying extremely well and there were plenty of them. One of the men was shooting in a particularly busy butt. In fact so many grouse were coming his way that he could barely reload quickly enough to keep pace with them. Then there was a long pause, which later on seemed strange given the pace at which the birds had consistently come until that moment. After he'd got his breath a most extraordinary thing happened. He was quite relaxed and standing, gun up, ready for whatever was to happen next when a single grouse appeared on the horizon and headed straight towards him.

Those who have been grouse shooting will realise that from the time a grouse appears to the time it has rocketed past you and out of sight is very short indeed. In this case the sportsman had no need to fire. Perhaps it was tiredness caused by the amount of shooting he'd already done, perhaps something else had distracted him, but whatever the reason he didn't fire, merely watching the grouse for the second it took to disappear. Just as that happened there was a terrific thump on the end of his gun and it was almost wrenched out of his hand. A second grouse had crashed into his barrels about halfway along and it lay stone dead in the grouse butt right at his feet.

The man dined out on the story for many years and even thought of having the bird stuffed – he was particularly taken by the whole thing as, thirty years earlier, his father had been shooting pheasants when a big cock bird crashed out of the sky and hit the stock of *his* gun which had been left lying on a straw bale. That pheasant had been killed instantly and the stock of an extremely valuable gun was smashed beyond repair.

TIGER AGAINST TIGER

INDIA, 1930

At Nundwass in India a local shikari or hunter spent the night waiting for a rogue tiger that had killed many local sheep and cows and had even tried to carry off a child. He was at the edge of a thick area of elephant grass where a buffalo had been killed the previous day by the rogue tiger – it had been an extraordinary battle as the buffalo had the initial luck to turn on the tiger rather than be attacked from behind by it. Effectively the buffalo kept the tiger at bay for some considerable time before a series of relatively minor wounds weakened it sufficiently for the tiger to move in for the kill. The noise of the battle had alerted the villagers who decided to scare the tiger off and then wait for it to return to its kill, by which time they would have a man with a gun in position.

The man chosen to shoot the tiger knew his best chance would come in the first hour after dawn and that is precisely what happened. From his vantage point in a tree he saw vague shadows as the tiger approached the carcase of the buffalo a little before first light. Then the hunter heard the tearing of flesh and crunching of bones as the tiger began to eat. Eagerly the hunter waited for enough light to shoot, but by the time he could see clearly he made an extraordinary discovery – as the first tiger tore at the buffalo it was itself being stalked by a second tiger and in the instant that the hunter saw the second animal it attacked. For almost half an hour the hunter watched the two tigers savagely attacking each other – an occurrence so rare as to be almost unheard of.

The first bouts were centred around the carcase of the buffalo, but as the battle became more savage the two animals gradually crashed and tumbled out of sight into the surrounding jungle, but for almost an hour more they could be heard roaring savagely. Then all was quiet. Either the tigers had both given up the struggle or one had been killed. The hunter waited till daylight to climb down from his perch in the tree and see exactly what had happened. To his astonishment he found both tigers dead within feet of each other – one was unmistakably the rogue animal that had been attacking the village.

ELEPHANT-RIDING TIGER

INDIA, 1930

Tiger shooting seems a pretty awful business today. Cruel, pointless and wasteful it may seem, but an earlier age viewed these things differently and tiger shooting, for good or ill, was one of those things that the travelling aristocratic Englishman always wanted to try.

Most accounts of tiger-shooting expeditions make pretty dull reading, but the account of Captain Forsyth, who was in India in the early 1930s, is by any standards exciting and extraordinary.

Traditionally the tiger-shooter would travel by elephant with a mahout – the controller of the elephant. The mahout would sit nearest the animal's head, the shooting man next and at the back another servant.

Captain Forsyth, the servant and the mahout had covered a great deal of ground on this particular day but without the least sniff of a tiger. Towards evening they had wandered into a narrow, densely forested area when their elephant paused and began to kick and paw the earth in a manner that indicated the certain presence of a tiger. Forsyth peered ahead but could make out nothing in the half-light. The mahout then said he thought he could see the tiger crouching in a dense bush. Forsyth threw a few large stones into the bush. The tiger immediately emerged roaring loudly and bolted through the bushes down a narrow ride. Unfortunately for the tiger another elephant had blocked that ride further off so it had to turn back. Captain Forsyth had a couple of shots at the tiger as it charged his elephant – he missed with both barrels and the elephant, which had been quiet and steady until now, began to lose its nerve. So much so that it spun round, almost unseating the captain, and presented its rear to the rapidly approaching tiger. As the captain later recalled, the elephant seemed to freeze and just in that moment the tiger leapt halfway up its back and dug its claws into the poor elephant's hide just to the side of its tail.

With all the coolness in the world the captain leaned back, pushed his rifle's muzzle over the elephant's haunches and with one hand shot the tiger dead. The elephant, which was called Sarju, knowing it was safe, immediately spun round and did a dance of victory on top of the body of its vanquished foe. Five minutes later there was very little of the tiger left and it had almost literally to be prised out of the sandy soil, as flat as a pancake.

TOOTHLESS TIGER

INDIA, 1930

Jim Corbett, who made his name with three books about life in India early in the twentieth century, was not a sentimental man, but he was one of the first to realise that it would probably not be a good idea to pursue and kill every big animal in Asia – a notion that would have seemed bizarre fifty years earlier.

Unlike many Victorian sportsmen, he also had a healthy respect for the environment in which he lived, but at the same time he knew that when he was out in the jungle the best way to survive was to live off the land and he regularly shot birds sitting – highly unsporting from the English gentleman's point of view – to make sure that valuable ammunition wasn't wasted on high-flying birds that were all too easy to miss. What is the point of good sport, he would have argued, when you end up with an empty stomach?

At the end of a long day shooting for pheasants and jungle fowl for his supper, Corbett began to make his way home with a few good birds in his bag. He was almost home when he was caught in a storm, but this was no ordinary storm. Corbett was in the foothills of the Himalayas, an area where the weather was often unpredictable, particularly when it had been dry for any length of time. The area had actually been drought-ridden for months so the storm he saw coming on the back of an inky-blue cloud was, he knew, likely to be ferocious, but even Corbett with his wide experience of India, could not have predicted what followed. Hailstones as big as eggs thundered out of the sky smashing into plants and trees and knocking birds of every description out of the sky. Crops were flattened and birds as big as vultures lay strewn across a broad swathe of land.

Corbett managed to avoid injury by getting quickly under cover, but he heard later from villagers that it was not uncommon for cattle, monkeys and even children to be killed by these hailstone storms.

Corbett was no stranger to extraordinary events and it was on a shooting expedition soon after the hailstone storm that he came across something equally remarkable. A buffalo had gone berserk in his local village causing a huge and damaging stampede of all the other buffalo in the herd. The villagers had eventually managed to shoot the maddened animal, but Corbett wanted to investigate the incident. He examined the dead animal and discovered that huge chunks of flesh had been torn from its back. There was no explanation for this, so Corbett laid baits for the culprit. A few nights later from his tree-top hiding place he saw a poorly nourished tiger attack the bait, but the tiger used only its claws to rip at the meat and Corbett saw that in some accident it had lost most of its lower jaw. Unable to use its jaws to throttle the buffalo in the normal way it had obviously leaped on to its back and begun eating the poor animal even as it ran off. Understandably the buffalo had panicked and in its panic-stricken charge it had caused a stampede of the whole herd.

DUCK SURPRISE

NORTH AMERICA, 1931

Just as the Great Depression in America was beginning, the number of rabbits, geese, deer and other game being pursued rose hugely as people tried to supplement drastically reduced or non-existent incomes. Americans always had widely different shooting traditions from their European cousins, the major difference being that in so big a country you could always wander about at will and shoot whatever you liked, because you were never likely to get in anyone else's way. Try that in crowded little England and you would very likely end up shooting a beater or the man behind the hedge in the next field.

Occasionally, of course, Americans do like to shoot together and at these times they no doubt do have rules and disciplines to prevent them filling each other with lead. But there are and always have been near misses, including some quite remarkable ones.

Two friends, a Mr Scott and Mr Simpson, were shooting ducks from what Americans call a double battery – a kind of tin boat affair anchored up offshore and containing coffinlike compartments in which the gunners lie until the game is in sight.

Anyway, our intrepid pair were out lying in their battery awaiting the dawn flight of duck. Surrounding their battery, and sprinkled as naturally here and there on the water as possible, were numerous wooden decoy duck floating realistically on the water.

The two men were on the Great South Bay, a noted wildfowl area. The technique adopted here is that the gunners lie concealed in their narrow compartments until they hear the duck alighting in and around the decoys. They then sit up, the duck rise from the water and the gunners open fire. All well and good.

The two men, exchanging occasional pleasantries and exhorting each other every now and then to be quiet, had been waiting for something to happen for over two hours when the whiffle of wings told them that a party of broadbills had arrived. The two men sat up simultaneously. The duck rose in a panic from the water and the two gunners fired one barrel each.

Mr Scott fired at a bird that had risen just a couple of feet from the water. At the same moment Mr Simpson fired at a bird well up in the air. Mr Scott was about to fire his second barrel when the bird he was aiming at crumpled and fell into the water. Yet Mr Scott knew he hadn't managed to fire at it. At the exact instant the bird crumpled Mr Scott felt a jarring in his gun as if it had been fired. But he knew he hadn't fired and on opening his gun he found, as he knew he would, the cartridge still intact. From the damage to his gun Mr Scott quickly realised what had happened. Just as he'd been about to fire at his low bird, Mr Simpson, swinging his gun to catch up with the higher bird had fired and hit Mr Scott's gun barrels about six inches from the muzzle. The shot struck the right barrel a glancing blow, broke through the wall of the barrel and then continued along the inside of that barrel and out the end. The gun being already aimed at a duck, the shot travelled out of the muzzle in exactly the right direction to bring down the bird that Mr Scott had been aiming at all the time.

GUINEA FOWL AND SNAKEBITE

LIBERIA, 1931

Ellis Briggs was for some time the United States' ambassador to the African state of Liberia. The first time the ambassador went shooting he and his party watched from their car the miles of equatorial forest on either side of the road to the interior until fifteen miles inland they came to a vast area of knee-high grass. The ambassador was convinced that a place like this must be full of game birds. The grass stretched for miles in every direction and locals told them that the area was absolutely seething with guinea fowl.

The ambassador was so optimistic about the whole enterprise that on his first day out he hired a whole team of assistants to carry home the huge numbers of birds he was sure he would bag.

Manpower was not a problem. Within hours of the ambassador's request for assistants going out he was inundated with Liberians from as far as fifteen miles away. He chose a dozen or so and set off for the savannah he had encountered that first day. The grass was indeed full of game birds, but it was also full of deadly mamba snakes and vipers. The shooting party did reasonably well, but not as well as they'd hoped, largely because every step was a nightmare of risk – tread unwarily on a snake and you would receive a potentially lethal bite.

They gave up and paid off their assistants, but determined to return with better clothing. A few days later, and this time with clothing more suited to the dangers of snakebite, they

273

returned to the savannah. This time the snakes were not going to be a problem but when they arrived they realised that word of the American guinea fowl shooters had crossed the country and there were so many people offering their services that not a blade of grass could be seen so great was the crowd. The savannah was a shambles and no game bird could have survived that deluge of feet for five miles in any direction.

It took a week for the excitement to die down and the ambassador's party had to hire a local man to organise the beaters and assistants. At last they managed to get to the savannah suitably dressed and with a reasonable number of beaters. The shooting was apparently extraordinary – the Liberian guinea fowl, a brown bird about the size of a grouse, is a fast-flying, extremely acrobatic bird with enough brains to stay on the ground and run for it unless it absolutely has to fly.

What impressed the ambassador most however, was not the quality of the shooting but the ability of the two dozen local beaters to walk through the dense grass without looking and with no shoes and yet not once get bitten by the vast numbers of snakes that seemed to be everywhere. The ambassador was enormously pleased at the thought that however many birds they shot they seemed to have no effect on the numbers of birds in the area.

Officials from the Monrovian embassy got to hear about the trips to the savannah and several cadged a lift with the American ambassador but they were so overexcited and unsafe that the invitation was not repeated – one Monrovian shot a hole in the floor of the car, another used the vast bulk of his cartridges on anything and everything that moved and had used most of them up within the first hour.

THE AEROPLANE BEATER

YORKSHIRE, 1932

Stanley Duncan was one of the best-known wildfowlers of the twentieth century, although his long career began in the nineteenth. He shot geese and duck all along the Wash and the Norfolk coast and elsewhere and became well known through his letters and articles in various magazines and newspapers. Perhaps his most extraordinary exploit came when he helped a pilot friend use an aeroplane to improve his goose shooting.

When October came the experiment began. A field in Yorkshire where the geese were known to feed regularly was left undisturbed for a few weeks to allow the birds to settle in. The geese that came in were watched continually and as many as twenty-four at a time were discovered. Duncan decided this was sufficient for his friend's experiment with the aeroplane. The idea was that the pilot would take off and then fly low over the hedge at the edge of the field where the geese were feeding. The plane, it was thought, would put the birds up, but would also drive them forward towards two guns waiting at the far end of the field.

The first attempt failed miserably. The plane buzzed over the hedge but the geese had clearly heard its engine long before it reached them and they flew almost vertically high into the sky, before swinging quickly away to the left long before the plane even arrived.

The pilot landed again. The two gunners got into position on the off chance that the birds would return. Two hours later some sixteen geese alighted on the field and began to feed. The wind had risen and this may have contributed to the fact that the birds, on the second attempt, did not hear the plane's engine until it was too late. The plane rushed over the hedge about sixty feet above the geese. The birds were apparently so astonished that they made no attempt to fly off and flattened themselves against the ground instead. One of the gunners fired and the geese got up and soared away downwind, but the presence of the plane kept them close to the ground. Some tumbled into a hedge bottom, others managed to gain height before the airman, turning quickly, got above the flock again pushing the geese towards the guns. At the end of the evening most of the flock had been bagged and the experiment was counted a success. For some reason, perhaps because it gave the birds so little chance, it was never repeated.

POACHER RACING

SCOTLAND, 1932

A keeper in the Highlands wandering his estate early one morning came across four poachers, each with a shotgun, and a fierce-looking lurcher. The keeper was alone, but Highland keepers are a breed apart and, despite the fact the poachers were already four hundred yards away when the keeper first shouted at them, he decided to give chase. Three of the four poachers were young and very fast, but the fourth clearly older and a great deal stockier than his friends, was a slow runner and the keeper began to catch up with him. Looking over his shoulder the stout poacher suddenly jettisoned a fat rabbit which came sailing over his head and almost hit the keeper in the face. Immediately the poacher picked up a bit of speed, but the keeper maintained his pace and began to gain on the man once again. The poacher, glancing once again over his shoulder, saw that he was in trouble again and immediately hurled an even bigger rabbit back over his shoulder towards the keeper. This was followed by two more rabbits and shortly thereafter by a hare. By this time the poacher had been transformed from a great fat lumbering thing into a lithe sprinter. The keeper having chased his man for more than half a mile gave up the chase and stooped to pick up the hare. As he did so the poacher's lurcher shot past his hand, picked up the hare in its mouth and started off towards its master. Enraged the keeper began once again to give chase. Two or three hundred yards further on the poacher again dropped the hare, but when the keeper tried to pick it up the lurcher managed to turn and snatch it up again just in time.

This happened several more times until, thoroughly exasperated, the keeper fired his shotgun at the lurcher's rear end. He was using only dust shot so the animal was not badly injured, but it was enough to ensure that the dog did not again return to pick up the hare.

The keeper knew the stout poacher well, but in the 1930s as now, it was a question of catching a poacher red-handed if anything was to be done, but having shot the man's dog the keeper knew the poacher would seek revenge. The poacher was apparently a noted local amateur boxer and so the keeper was not surprised late one night on his way home from the pub to see a figure lurch out from the hedgerow and aim a sharp blow at his head.

What the boxing poacher did not know was the keeper was himself a former champion wrestler. In the pitched battle that followed the poacher must have been astonished to find his every blow skilfully parried and to realise he was not going to come off best. In fact, within minutes the poacher had been hurled to the ground where he was kept pinned until a policeman had been called.

After paying his fine in the local magistrates court a few weeks later, the poacher shook hands with the keeper, said there were no hard feelings and that they might have a pint together next time they met in the Wagon and Horses.

GIANT FROGS

PERU, 1935

The American ambassador to Peru in the 1930s was asked by a friend to collect half a dozen Andean bullfrogs – giant creatures as much as two feet long and weighing several pounds. They were wanted alive but when the ambassador said he would try to collect them he was also told that in the area where they were to be found, there was excellent duck shooting.

The ambassador was Ellis Briggs, a keen sportsman who had shot all over the world – wherever in fact his duties as an ambassador took him.

The ambassador took a party of his friends in search of the frogs which were believed to be most abundant where the river Mantaro became broader and slower flowing at about eleven thousand feet above sea level. Along the river at this point the railway ran parallel for miles so the party decided to take the train and hop off to look for frogs at every likely looking spot.

The lure of frogs was really a bit of an excuse for the fabulous duck shooting the area was supposed to offer, so they took care to take their guns and plenty of ammunition.

But word had got out that these American frog hunters would be coming to the area and, on the day they took the train, wherever they stopped hundreds of local people gathered in the hope of being taken on as beaters or assistants. In fact there were so many that any self-respecting frog would long ago have vanished. It was the same wherever the train stopped and no amount of shouting at the locals would make them go away. Eventually they did manage to shake off their followers and they netted the reed beds and shallow margins of the river. The area was, as they had been told, alive with giant Andean bullfrogs. They caught twenty-eight in total and named the biggest – which measured just over two feet from tip of nose to tip of extended feet – Reginald. In between keeping an eye out for the huge numbers of teal and other ducks said to inhabit the area, the ambassador's party had the sense to collect sackfuls of live insects – essential if the frogs were to survive the boat trip back to the United States. But after all their efforts and success with both frogs and insects not a single duck showed up.

The ambassador heard several weeks later that all but five of the frogs had arrived safely in the United States, although they'd had to feed them cockroaches towards the end of their journey as the greedy amphibians had demolished the captured insects at an astonishing rate. Then his informant confided that although they'd arrived in the States the frogs hadn't got beyond the pier at New Orleans because their papers were not in order. Eventually the harbour master had agreed that they could go to the zoo. Five had died on the journey so that left twenty-three frogs, but the zoo had only taken sixteen. The rest apparently ended up in the local restaurant where a favoured diner commented on the magnificence of the frogs' legs he ate that night.

BULLFIGHTER

ESSEX, 1938

Before artificial insemination, high-tech farming and improved rural transport, bulls were a serious menace in the countryside because virtually every farmer with cattle needed the services of a bull. Ramblers and walkers were regularly attacked; sometimes they were injured, occasionally even killed. Those who went shooting had fewer problems because they were usually locals and they knew pretty much the temperament and whereabouts of every bull. Occasionally, of course, the system broke down as it did early one morning on the marshes of the Essex coast.

Two gunners crossing a field with a bag of rabbits and duck in the autumn of 1938 saw a bull detach itself from a herd of cows about three hundred yards away. Having moved away from the rest of the animals the bull simply stopped and stared. To the experienced bull watcher this was the first very serious sign that they were in trouble. A moment later the bull went down on its knees and began churning up great clods of earth. This was a very bad sign indeed. The bull got up and began a steady trot toward the two men. They began to run towards a distant gate. After twenty feet one of the men tripped over an ant hill and went sprawling.

By the time he'd got back on his feet, three-quarters of a ton of angry bull was coming towards him at twenty miles an hour, head down and making the ground shake. With the bull just seventy odd yards away one of the shooters shouted to the other, 'Let the bugger have it!' Knowing there was nothing else he could do the man who'd fallen fired his 10-bore straight at the bull's lowered head. The shot, which probably did little real harm, made the bull turn on a sixpence and head at top speed for the sea wall some three-quarters of a mile away.

Another old marsh gunner whose antics with angry bulls were recalled by the writer James Wentworth Day was Ted Allen. His technique with a bull that looked in the least belligerent was not to run away, but to run right up to it. He'd then get down on his hands and knees and begin digging up great clods of mud and grass and throwing these at the bull's head. Baffled at this strange bull-like behaviour from something that didn't look in the least bovine, the bull would hesitate, at which point Ted Allen would rush up to it and clout it on the nose with his walking stick. At that the bull would retreat as fast as its legs could carry it.

TIGER ZENITH

NEPAL, 1938

Tiger shooting in India and Nepal probably reached its zenith in the 1920s and 1930s. Certainly during this period it was not uncommon to kill a dozen or more animals in a day and somehow those who hunted the tiger managed to convince themselves that they could carry on indefinitely at this rate.

On an extraordinary day in 1938 a party of hunters, headed by the maharajah of Nepal, who was a passionate tiger hunter, killed over forty tigers. The hunt was organised in a most extraordinary way and in a way that was unique to Nepal. Dozens of highly trained elephants with hunters on their back would gradually encircle a part of the jungle where there were numerous tigers. As the circle of elephants moved in on itself long stretches of white canvas would be stretched between them by beaters walking just behind the elephants. This meant that at a certain point, two or three or perhaps as many as a dozen tigers would be trapped inside a circle of canvas and elephants. As the tigers dashed about trying to look for a way out the hunters mounted on the elephants would take shots at them.

It must have been a pretty sorry affair and it is difficult today to do anything other than sympathise with the tigers which had almost no chance of escape. So goaded were they sometimes that they would simply run at an elephant and try to attack it and, of course, as soon as they did that they would be shot. However, it says much for the then abundance of tigers that for several decades they were able to survive hunting at this level.

283

BIRD ATTACK

WALES, 1946

Two Welsh farmers were out shooting just after the war. It was a wonderfully crisp autumn day, the trees still in leaf, but turning here and there into every conceivable shade of red, brown and yellow.

They'd just emerged through a narrow gap in a thick, well-grown hedge when they disturbed a hare just a few yards ahead of them. Up got the hare at a terrific speed and tore across the field away from the two sportsmen. Then, to their astonishment, the hare collided with a rabbit that was racing for its burrow under the hedge. The thwack of the two animals colliding was clearly audible and for a moment both lay completely still. Before the two farmers had a chance to do anything other than gape in astonishment the hare staggered to its feet, shook itself and limped away as if completely drunk. The rabbit never got up again. When the two farmers arrived at the scene it was stone dead.

At lunch the two farmers hadn't fired a shot, but they had that one rabbit in the bag and were looking forward to better luck in the afternoon.

Seeing two animals run into each other at high speed is and was a rare occurrence so the two farmers were probably thinking nothing else unusual would happen on that day but, remarkably, they were wrong. An hour after lunch they'd bagged another rabbit and a couple of pheasants and were feeling a little happier. One of the farmers always tried to take home a few pigeon as his wife was particularly fond of them, so he was delighted when a good fat pigeon rose out of a nearby copse and headed rapidly towards him at an eminently shootable height. With little trouble he knocked the bird out of the sky and it landed some distance away, but as the farmer went to collect the bird he felt something whoosh close above his head. He ducked and before he had time to wonder what was going on something really did hit him. He later swore it was a red kite, but whatever it was, it was certainly an angry bird of prey that mobbed about his head every time he tried to walk over to pick up his pigeon.

Astonished, the farmer gave up and quickly retreated. After one or two more half-hearted swoops at his head, the kite or whatever it was seemed to calm down and it then left him alone. A few moments later the kite swooped on the pigeon, took a few bites out of it and then flew off. The two men waited to see if it would return but it was clearly happy with its free lunch. The pigeon was now a sorry mess and not worth taking home, but as one farmer said to the other: 'How many men have seen two such extraordinary incidents in one day?'

CRAFTY KEEPER

SCOTLAND, 1946

At the end of a most successful shooting day just after the war the local vicar – who was one of the shoot's keenest participants – approached the keeper and asked him why he had not been to church for so long.

'Well,' said the crafty keeper, 'I don't come to church for a very good reason – it's out of pure consideration for yourself.'

'What on earth do you mean?' came the amazed reply.

'Well, it's like this,' said the keeper. 'If I go to church on a Sunday the whole parish will know it and they'll all go poaching since I'm the only man can stop them. If I stay away none of the men of the village will dare to go poaching so they might as well go to church, which they do. If I turn up to church you'll be preaching to empty pews, so I dare not do it.'

With that the keeper broke away and carried on loading the game cart. The parson, sensible enough to know when he'd been out manoeuvred, beat a hasty retreat.

STALKER'S GHOST

INVERNESS, 1947

A crofter living on a remote mountainside well to the north of Inverness was well situated in the middle of an area where there were large numbers of red deer. Every now and then he would go out and shoot one, largely because he enjoyed venison, but also because he enjoyed the great difficulty of stalking these easily spooked animals and getting within range for a shot.

Over a period of several months he'd seen a particularly fine stag with a really good head and he decided that, for the head alone, he would stalk and shoot the animal. He was an enormously experienced stalker so he knew he would get his stag sooner or later.

He set off and took a long way round to where he thought the stag was lying in order to be always downwind of it. After several hours he'd managed to get within a few hundred yards of the animal, although not quite close enough for a shot. What the crofter didn't know was that a local landowner was also stalking the very same stag, but from a completely different angle. The second stalker spotted the crofter and decided on a whim not to continue his pursuit of the stag, but – for the fun of it – to see if he could stalk the crofter.

Just as the crofter had selected a grassy knoll from which to take his shot, the second stalker had almost caught up with him. The crofter crouching quietly behind the knoll perhaps only eighty yards from the stag paused to catch his breath. He placed his rifle on the ground by his side while he got out his monocular to take one last look and check the exact position of the stag. Running right by the grassy knoll was a narrow burn that was almost dry for there had been little rain for weeks. The second stalker had wormed his way along this dried-up watercourse and while the crofter was making his last few observations over the top of the grassy knoll the second stalker carefully pushed his hand up through the bracken and stole the crofter's rifle.

Satisfied with his position and that of the stag, the stalker put his hand down to the place where he had left his rifle and of course it was gone. He scrabbled around desperately thinking, 'This is impossible.'

After a few seconds, during which time seemed to hang suspended in the air, a deep sepulchral voice sounded as if from the very depths of the earth.

'Donald, where's your rifle!'

Horrified, Donald sprang to his feet, regardless of the deer or anything and ran for his life, never stopping until he'd reached his own door. It was a long time before he ventured out in pursuit of deer again.

SHOOTING WITH THE SECRET SERVICE

CZECHOSLOVAKIA, 1949

In Communist Czechoslovakia, where the American ambassador Ellis Briggs was stationed for some time, there came each year to the American embassy an invitation to shoot. For a keen shooting man like the ambassador it was difficult to resist because the venue was the old Hapsburg hunting lodge at Zidlochovice.

Each gun was told to bring at least 800 rounds of ammunition – the communists were going to show these Americans that the Czechs could produce a much bigger and therefore better shoot than any decadent capitalist.

Zidlochovice, some 150 miles east of Prague, had for centuries been the sporting preserve of the Hapsburg kings. It was famous for huge bags of pheasants and for being close to the site of the Battle of Austerlitz, which was fought just a little beyond the end of the vast estate forests.

The lodge at Zidlochovice was monumental in scale and also monumentally uncomfortable – too cold in winter, too hot in summer. Every room – and the rooms were vast – was filled with trophies. It was almost as if the communists had to outdo their aristocratic hunting forebears. Bad-tempered looking statues of Stalin were everywhere among the wall-to-wall deer trophies, almost as if the heads were not deer at all but the heads of his victims.

As it turned out, the day's shooting was as vast as the lodge and as uncomfortable. It was also run with absurdly militaristic precision. A trumpeter blasted the guests out of bed at 6 a.m. and the ambassador had a sense of foreboding when he shouldered his bag of 800 cartridges – it was almost too heavy for one man to carry at all, let alone comfortably.

A speech filled with stern warnings was designed to ensure that the guns knew what they could and could not do – the threat of the Gulag seemed to hang over everything – and then they were off.

Each shoot day of the season involved using at least 300 local farmer beaters and there were so many shoot days that the estate produced more than forty thousand birds a season – a figure that would be an embarrassment for any English shoot.

The American ambassador noticed as they gathered outside the lodge that there were secret policeman everywhere. They hadn't even had the sense to change out of their cheap city overcoats and city shoes which were already stained badly with mud. The American ambassador thought they seemed extremely ill at ease, probably because here at least they could not arrest anyone for subverting the aims of the revolution (or whatever) simply because all those doing the shooting were diplomats with diplomatic immunity.

Each man shooting was supplied with a man to carry his guns, another man to carry his cartridges and a boy with a pad and pencil to keep his score. Each man shooting also had a team of three city-dressed secret service men attached to him.

They were warned not to shoot boar or deer, but anything else was fair game and then it was time for the off – or at least it was time once the officials had persuaded the Argentine ambassador that he would not need his revolver.

There were ten diplomats shooting and they were taken to a section of forest where ten dark rides were cut through the trees before disappearing over the horizon. Ambassadors got the best lanes (the ones in the middle) while lesser-ranking officials were assigned to the outer rides. As the guns walked along their rides there would be dozen of beaters keeping pace with them on either side through the thick woods putting the birds up – at least that was the theory.

Then the ambassador realised that so obsessed with control were the officials that he was to be allowed only to shoot when his loader decided to load the gun. When he asked if he could perform this little task for himself it was made abundantly clear that this would not be acceptable.

The incongruous little group moved off into their ride and perhaps at some unseen signal from the secret service men, the ambassador's gun bearer suddenly took two cartridges from the ammunition man. He loaded the gun and handed it to the ambassador. A pheasant got up a few yards further on and the gun bearer, the scorer, the ammunition carrier and the secret service policemen all bellowed 'Shoot!'

Flustered by the roars of the crowd the ambassador missed and the scorer shouted 'Zero' and marked the poor man's scorecard appropriately.

Several similar shots followed and, though rattled by the extraordinary circumstances in which he found himself, the ambassador eventually managed to shoot a hen pheasant. He was then told that hens were not allowed and he was told much as a naughty five-year-old would be told off for failing to tidy his bedroom.

And so it continued for mile after mile through the forest. The ambassador was never allowed to handle a single cartridge and he had to endure a permanent and voluble audience of six who screamed either 'Zero!' or 'Hen' or 'Don't shoot!' at every opportunity.

The loudest shouts came from the three secret service policemen.

The ambassador, too diplomatic to say anything, was beginning to get extremely annoyed, particularly at the three secret service policemen who looked out of place and were easily the most annoying members of an incredibly annoying group.

The ambassador decided to teach the spooks a lesson. When a hare ran on ahead of him he paused, hoping the hare would do that strange thing that driven hares often do – double back on itself. Clearly the gods were with the ambassador, for having run fifty feet forward the hare did a U-turn and ran back and almost through the ambassador's legs. He waited until it had reached the three secret service policemen and, knowing full well that shooting behind was not permitted, turned and fired between the second and the third policemen and well above the hare's head.

The policemen threw themselves on the ground while the scorer shouted, 'Good shooting!'

But the shot had the desired effect. The policemen kept much further back and made no further comment on the ambassador's shooting.

A little more relaxed by now, the ambassador got into his swing and when the walked-up shooting was over and the guns tried shooting from pegs he knocked thirty-eight birds out of the sky in just fifteen minutes. But as he said later, this was not actually that much of an achievement as the sky was continually black with birds.

At the end of that one day ten diplomats had shot 1,450 pheasants, together with 700 hares and more than 300 rabbits. Several of the diplomats, who had fired almost continually for more than five hours, had smashed fingers, dislocated arms and severe shoulder bruising.

Most of the game from Zidlochovice was not, sadly, sent off to be consumed by the workers in distant factories and farms – it was sent to the West as quickly as possible in exchange for hard currency. But on the day of the ambassador's shoot the officials insisted that all the game belonged to the people of Czechoslovakia and that it was going to the West because that was the will of the people.

THE RAISIN TRICK

DEVON, 1950

Pheasant shooting has always been expensive. It's not just the cost of guns and cartridges – pheasants take a lot of looking after if they are to survive to adulthood. Feed is expensive, as is the cost of keeping fox numbers under control, so when that bird finally takes to the air it represents a heavy investment for someone, which is why those who shoot driven pheasants regularly tend to be rather well off. But not always.

A farm worker in Devon who was well known locally as a bit of a character and who went beating regularly on neighbouring farms and estates, always complained that the only pheasant shooting he ever got was one day at the end of the season when all the guns on his main shoot changed places with the beaters. On this one day each year the beaters got to shoot while the guns did the beating.

But William wasn't happy with this. He wanted to be able to shoot pheasants whenever he fancied, but he couldn't afford it and that seemed to be that. Then he had a brainwave. He lived at the end of a long track at the edge of a wood and visitors were a rarity. This was in the early 1950s when North Devon was still a remote place and ramblers and day-trippers were still almost unheard of.

Will knew a great deal about pheasants as he'd been involved with them one way and another since he was a boy. He knew every trick in the book, including a poacher's trick he'd occasionally used as a boy when his father had lost his job and Will and his brothers and sisters found themselves with nothing in the house for supper.

Will remembered that on these occasions he'd taken a few raisins out into the neighbouring wood and laid a trail from a likely looking bit of the wood – preferably near a pheasant pen – back to his own cottage garden. Where the trail ended in the garden a box would be propped up on a stick and a little pile of raisins left underneath it. A fine length of fishing line led from the stick into the house where the young Will would sit absolutely still for hours waiting his chance.

Eventually a pheasant would find the first few raisins back in the wood and begin to follow them. Soon he would arrive in the cottage garden, wander under the box and Will would give a smart tug on the line. Supper was no longer a problem.

Will recalled these early days and thought he would adapt the raisin technique to his current need for his very own low-cost personal pheasant shoot. He began to lay raisin trails all over the adjacent wood, which was a heavily stocked commercial shoot. The one thing the hundred-odd raisin trails had in common was that they all led back to Will's garden.

He didn't know whether it would work – perhaps 1950s pheasants were wiser than their counterparts fifty years earlier, but Will would give it a try come what may.

In the days following his trail-laying, Will noticed that there was a steady flow of birds into the garden. They hung around for a while and then gradually disappeared. On the Friday of the first week of the new season he went out and relaid his raisin trail and then set up a comfortable chair in his garden, with the cottage behind and a few straw bales in front of his position. When he sat in his chair the straw bales would conceal him from any pheasants that had entered the garden.

On the Saturday he leaped out of bed dressed in his warmest clothes, cleaned and oiled his gun and made sure he had plenty of cartridges. He sat behind his straw bales with a hot cup of tea and awaited events. Fifteen minutes later the shooting began. Will got his gun ready and without peering over the top of the straw bales he stood up. Three pheasants saw him and took off immediately like rockets. As they headed towards the trees Will achieved a very fine right and left. He sent his dog to retrieve the two birds, chuckling to himself the whole time. At the end of the day he'd shot more than twenty pheasants and was delighted with the success of his plan. He knew he couldn't be accused of poaching as he'd shot the birds on his own land and pheasants, like other game birds, were classed as wild and therefore not owned by anyone other than the person whose land they happened to be on at any one time.

He was convinced that nothing could go wrong. He could enjoy a bit of pheasant shooting every day if he liked and he wouldn't have to beat for anyone ever again.

The only problem was that he had to trespass to leave his trail of raisins but that just couldn't be helped. He'd have to take the risk and if he didn't overdo it he'd be fine. On a really big estate like the one next door they'd never notice a few missing pheasants anyway.

Alas for Will, the keeper on the adjacent shoot did notice something funny going on. There were a lot of pheasants it is true, but the keeper was as much of an old hand as Will and he knew they were disappearing a little faster than they should be, so he decided to investigate. It didn't take him long to realise that those occasional shots every other Saturday were coming from a garden just on the edge of the estate, and he even spent some time watching from a discreet distance. He saw the birds falling, but what could he do? They were certainly his birds but that crafty old man was shooting them from his garden. The keeper spent weeks thinking about this and eventually sent a letter round to Will at his cottage.

'Hope you're enjoying good sport this year,' the keeper's letter read, 'but we've had poachers over here and our birds are disappearing so I just thought I should warn you not to let your dog stray over the boundary. We wouldn't want to shoot it in mistake for a poacher's dog.'

Will knew he'd been rumbled and, as most of the pheasants he'd been shooting in his garden, had to be retrieved from outside the garden he knew his crafty little private shoot would have to come to an end.

But this being a quiet country district no one wanted to upset anyone else more than was absolutely necessary, so when Will reappeared at the shoot offering to beat the following Saturday it was simply assumed that he'd been a little under the weather and was now back with his friends. And only Will noticed the sly wink the keeper gave him.

SWAN SONG

KOREA, 1950

Eating sandwiches and sipping Jack Daniels whiskey in the Korean countryside was one of the few real pleasures of being America's ambassador to that particular country in the 1950s. One day the ambassador was asked if he'd like to try to shoot a wild swan. These were hugely prolific around the estuary of the Naktong River, along whose sides the rice paddies spread as far as the eye could see.

As the ambassador and half a dozen friends waited, guns in their cases nearby, but relaxed and enjoying their Asian picnic, they heard far away the deep and unmistakable booming and trumpeting of the swans. Looking down the hillside on which they lay and away out towards the Naktong Delta, they thought they could just glimpse against the intense blue sky tiny movements high up.

The trumpeting grew louder. These were wild swans flying south from the ice-bound Siberian winter. In this quiet corner of Korea they spent their time feeding out at sea during the daytime and then flying back in the evening to the estuary to roost.

The shooters watched the birds land on the distant estuary and decided to try for them.

When they reached the sea their Korean guide told them to fan out along the sea wall. He would then move to a suitable position to fire at the swans and put them up off the lake and over towards the rest of the guns. He warned the Americans

297

that the birds would circle and then head for the sea, which should bring them within range.

When he was asked if he'd ever attempted to shoot swans over the estuary the guide admitted he had tried it on several occasions but they'd never bagged a swan.

Peeping over the sea wall the ambassador could see more than two hundred magnificent swans on the water, and no doubt he felt a pang of guilt about what they were about to do, but then shooting swans was perfectly legal in Korea and ideas about the rights of animals and conservation were still at least a decade away.

Suddenly they heard the sound of rifle fire and the great birds were moving clumsily but with increasing speed along the water and up into the air in their V-shaped flying formation. With every wingbeat they climbed higher into the crisp blue sky. As they passed over the ambassador and his fellow guns there was a volley of shots, but the great birds carried on unmolested.

A voice shouted: 'My God, those birds must have been five hundred feet up! We'd need anti-aircraft fire to hit them.'

But though they had all missed they found their guide half a mile away with a massive and very dead swan. By a million to one chance the shot he'd fired to put the swans up off the water had skimmed like a flat pebble and hit the swan sideways on, killing it instantly.

CHEEKY FOX

BUCKINGHAMSHIRE, 1951

At a Buckinghamshire shoot in the 1950s pheasants began to go missing. The problem wasn't poachers at night or on Sundays or other days when no legal shooting was taking place. The poaching appeared to be going on under the very noses of the guns on days when the shooting was perfectly legitimate. Two drives situated quite close to each other seemed to have the worst problems. At the end of a day at either or both of these drives the marked birds would be picked up by the labradors and spaniels. But far fewer birds were being gathered than seemed to have been hit.

At first the shoot owners and keepers thought it was just that the guns were over-optimistic in their estimates of what had been brought down, but even well-known and reliable teams were reporting twenty or more birds where only fifteen or so would be picked up. Then towards the end of the season, on a particularly good day, the mystery was solved.

One of the guns was absentmindedly watching a point at the end of a field where many of the birds tended to come down if they'd been shot. He watched in amazement as a fox appeared as if from nowhere, grabbed a bird and then within seconds vanished. When he went over to the place and looked carefully around he discovered that the fox had been hiding in a covered drain. It had learned that whenever there was a lot of noise in this place it was well worthwhile hiding in the ditch and then jumping out every now and then. Pheasants that did not run or fly away were raining out of the sky and from the fox's point of view this was manna from heaven. Curiously, once the fox's little plan had been uncovered the pheasants stopped disappearing and the fox was never seen again.

SHOOTING FROM A HELICOPTER

KOREA, 1951

The American ambassador Ellis Briggs seems to have worked in every country where it was worth working if you happened to be a keen shooting man – South America, Europe and most places in between. But Korea, despite the war going on at the time, seems to have been something special. Apart from a fascinating trip in search of wild swans, Korea gave him the chance to try out some novel not to say bizarre shooting techniques – top of the list in terms of sheer eccentricity has to be the time he organised a group of helicopters to drive duck.

This started out as a scientific study into a new cold-weather suit developed by the United States military. The ambassador seems to have got sufficiently involved with the project to try out the suit. It was made of what seemed to be foam rubber and plastic and, like a wetsuit, it was skintight and covered the wearer from ankle to neck. And however cold the weather, the suit was supposed to be sufficient protection on its own, or at least that was the theory.

Immediately he tried on the suit the ambassador found it was like being in an oven – which should not have been a problem as the suit was fitted with numerous ingenious vents.

However, the real test of the suit was to be conducted along Korea's Han River, a place of extreme cold in winter. The idea was to fly the ambassador and one or two other top officials – also dressed in the new suit – by helicopter, which was the only way into the area at that time. In return for testing the suit the ambassador persuaded the military authorities to let him try shooting duck out of the window of the helicopter.

301

The theory was this. You sat in the helicopter's plastic bubble – in other words in the main body of the thing – but with the right door removed. The pilot flew along until the chopper was alongside a cruising flock of mallard and the ambassador would then try to shoot them. If a duck went down the helicopter would land to pick it up.

When the three helicopters arrived in the Han Valley the men trying out the suits would be dropped on a giant ice floe where they would be left for several hours to test the suits. While they waited to be picked up the idea was that they would amuse themselves by shooting at any passing duck.

As the ambassador boarded his helicopter he was told by the pilot not to shoot upwards or to take any shots when either of the other helicopters was alongside. High shots, as the pilot pointed out, would make nasty holes in the helicopter's rotor blades, which might mean an unscheduled and very rapid descent. Those who'd shot from the chopper before – or so the ambassador was told – normally stepped partly out of the helicopter and put one foot on its ski. The ambassador thought he might give this technique a miss.

They took off, flying two hundred feet above the river. Soon they were matching the speed of a good flock of duck, but try as he might the ambassador couldn't hit a thing. He tried shooting further and further ahead of the lead duck hoping to allow for the speed of the helicopter, but it was no good.

At the end of the day he talked to a colonel who regularly shot duck from the helicopter and was told that he should have fired about one hundred feet ahead of any duck to have the least chance of hitting it. Theoretically this should not have been necessary as duck and helicopter were travelling at the same speed, but the problem was a mystery that would never be solved. The ambassador resolved to give it another go if the chance ever arose – it never did. But the trip hadn't been entirely wasted. He was able to report that the Michelin-man suit he'd been trying out was unbearably hot and was likely to be a complete waste of time anywhere other than at the South Pole.

BATTLES WITH THE CROCS

NEW GUINEA, 1952

Gunther Bahnemann was probably one of the last men to believe that the only good crocodile is a dead one. He went on several crocodile-hunting expeditions to New Guinea and seems to have felt that it would have been a good idea if every crocodile still left alive in the world at that time could be wiped out. His view seems based on the premise that crocodiles are cold killers, monsters from prehistoric times that have no place in the modern world. Ignorant of the crocodile's part in the food chain and its important role as part of the balancing mechanism of river systems, Bahnemann was nonetheless excellent at chronicling the role of the professional crocodile hunter. He poached crocodiles for their skins in the early 1950s in New Guinea despite the fact that it was completely illegal. Somehow he managed to avoid getting caught by the authorities and his descriptions of crocodile shooting are both gruesome and compelling.

He describes how on one expedition with a team of half a dozen local tribesmen – described by Bahnemann as 'savages' – he had managed to corner several crocodiles. It was already dark but the red of the crocodiles' eyes could be seen in the boat's powerful searchlights. In fact the searchlights had mesmerised the crocodiles and as long as they flickered over them the giant animals remained in their positions. Bahnemann or his partner would then shoot the crocodiles. As soon as they'd done so one of the tribesmen would throw a harpoon with a rope attached. If this stuck in a crocodile it would be hauled towards the boat and then finally killed with a blow from a hatchet. After one or two crocodiles had been killed like this the low-sided boat would be covered with blood and bone.

Despite several bullets, a harpoon and a hatchet blow the crocodiles often continued to fight. When this happened the croc would beat the water with its tail until spray was pouring over the men in the boat. The harpoon staves would be splintered into matchwood and the crocodile, as much as eighteen feet long, would roll over and over snapping its jaws again and again. A hand or leg anywhere near was in danger of being amputated in a second and the men would scatter quickly to the side of the boat opposite that at which the crocodile was performing its gymnastics. They would also try to move the end of the boat away from the tail in case it was splintered.

Bahnemann would then brace himself against a strut as the boat rocked dangerously and fire again and again at the twisting animals. He was frequently astonished at how long it took them to die. It is easy to imagine the chaos that must have ensued – the boat almost in darkness, apart from the thin beam from the searchlights, the crocodile half under the water and half concealed in reeds and mud thrashing blindly, the boat twisting and turning.

The crocodiles almost had their revenge one morning at dawn when Bahnemann fired at a croc that proved to have more energy than any Bahnemann had ever encountered. With a massive heave it hurled itself from the water, huge jaws snapping wildly. With paws beating the air it then stood vertically on its tail at the stern of the boat. Sitting in the firing chair on the boat Bahnemann had to lean back to keep away from the croc. There was no time for a shot as the crocodile crashed full length across the stern of the boat, smashing one of the searchlights and badly damaging the deck planking. The boat began to sink. Stuck in his chair and sprawled backwards, Bahnemann's feet were just inches from the crocodile's snapping jaws. He threw his rifle to his partner, but the only remaining headlight – at the wrong end of the boat – was pointing the wrong way. In the near darkness the boat was chaos with men rushing here and there in a bedlam of confusion made worse by the surface of the deck, which was covered with blood from stem to stern. Bahnemann couldn't get out of his seat without putting his feet in the crocodile's mouth. Its body was wedged on the boat so there was no chance of it sliding back into the water. Then there was a huge flash and a gun went off. Bahnemann felt the bullet hurtle past his head and into the crocodile, but despite being hit the croc simply redoubled its convulsive thrashing.

Bahnemann's partner was lying on his back hanging on to the boat rail and trying to aim his rifle with one hand. On the opposite side away from the crocodile two terrified tribesman hung on to the boat rail, which was nearly three feet in the air as the boat had sunk so far down on the other side.

Then somehow the crocodile got its head free and managed to sink its teeth into the three-inch-thick support rail that Bahnemann had been holding. It splintered like matchwood. Without this Bahnemann began to slide toward the crocodile's mouth. With a few inches to go he was caught by a wildly waving crocodile paw and knocked flat on the deck. As the croc continued to thrash its head from side to side a chunk of wood that had been sticking out of its mouth flew off and by an amazing chance hit the throttle on the boat's control console. The engine roared and the boat leaped forward knocking one man straight into the water. This movement gave Bahnemann enough time to get his revolver out of his holster. He fired nine times in less than three seconds and the crocodile died. He then managed to twist around and turn off the throttle. The engine faded and they took stock of the destruction. To get the boat back on an even keel, they had to chop the crocodile into two pieces. Only then could it be disentangled from the boat's structure and slid into the water.

The man who'd fallen in the water emerged unscathed, looked at the head end of the crocodile, which remained on the boat and said: 'Him proper bad bastard.'

The bravery of the local tribesmen can be judged by the fact that one of them immediately dived into the water, swam ten feet down and tied a noose round the body of the croc so it could be retrieved. The crocodile measured sixteen feet with a girth of fifty-nine inches. They sold the skin for twenty-six pounds and ten shillings and someone somewhere is probably still carrying a bag or a suitcase made from that doughty fighter.

SHOOT YOUR OWN PET

LINCOLNSHIRE, 1952

The writer and artist Denys Watkins Pitchford, better known as BB, started wildfowling – duck and goose shooting over estuaries and mudflats – when he was in his teens, and he was still making the long arduous journey from his home in Northamptonshire to the Solway Firth a few weeks before he died aged eighty-five in 1990. BB was an unusual man in many respects. He never went to school, but learned to read at an early age and spent much of his youth wandering the fields and hedgerows shooting and fishing with just a dog for company.

But BB had no interest in what he called the numbers game – in other words he loved shooting but disliked driven shoots where the guns were driven from drive to drive and might easily shoot two or three hundred birds in a day. BB liked to shoot alone or with a friend and he liked to cover plenty of ground in a day with just an occasional shot. Everything he shot he ate. He loved the idea of living off the land. But he could be surprisingly sentimental about the birds and animals that regularly fell to his gun. The story of his pet goose is a case in point.

BB had gone shooting on the Wash in Lincolnshire, one of the most desolate and dangerous places in Britain; a place where no shooter would dare go without a local guide, for the vast areas of mudflats are incredibly treacherous at the best of times. Take the wrong route across the featureless mud and there is a good chance you will vanish forever into twenty feet of sticky mud or the mist will come down and you'll find yourself suddenly surrounded by water as the tide creeps silently in around you.

BB always took a guide although he probably knew the Wash as well as any outsider. He was shooting in the early morning hoping to catch the geese on their dawn flight. He'd watched the light grow in intensity until, almost imperceptibly, the details round about became clear and it was morning. Then he heard the unmistakable sound of the geese coming towards him. Looking up he saw they were well within range and almost instinctively he fired, bringing one of the tail-enders down well behind him.

BB knew that at best he'd winged the bird. By the time he caught up with it the goose, which was a big one, was in a furious mood. It didn't try to run off, but with one wing clearly broken it merely hissed at BB. Under other circumstances BB might have grabbed it and simply knocked it on the head or if it had been able to run he might have had another shot at it. For some reason this time he didn't. He was never really able to explain why, but he made a grab at the bird and tucked it under one arm. No one knows what his guide made of this, but he carried the goose back to the car and took it home where he nursed it for several weeks. The bird made a complete recovery and became one of BB's best friends. It lived for many years and was, claimed BB, the best guard dog he ever had. Curiously the goose was easily tamed and the experience of getting to know a creature that had been intended for the pot never made a dent in BB's enthusiasm for shooting.

SKULL-BITER

NORFOLK, 1953

Short-un Page was born of a long line of wildfowlers. He was definitely not one of those gentlemen gunners who took up the sport in this century simply to impress their friends. Page's family had to harvest the wild geese and ducks to keep body and soul together in a harsh flat landscape where there was little else to do. Short-un helped his father, a professional wildfowler, from his earliest childhood, but at the age of about sixteen he decided to go it alone. He took off in his father's punt one icy day in 1953 and sculled up to Breydon. He had aboard his father's flintlock punt gun. It was ten feet long and carried nearly five ounces of shot. The force of the blast when he fired it would push the boat several yards back through the water and that massive charge of shot might take out a hundred birds at a time – birds that would end up in the London markets next morning.

Short-un's first day shooting alone was to become a thing of legend. With his first shot he knocked down five Brent geese. Shot number two brought him five curlew and his final shot, at the end of a day that left his hands so numb they would barely move, killed one hundred and fifty waders and five wigeon.

The wounded waders Short-un killed as did all the old gunners – by biting their skulls. When he rowed into port that evening children ran from him as from a ghost as his face was covered with the blood of knot, dunlin, and plover.

309

HOW THE HUNTERS DO IT

NEW GUINEA, 1954

On a crocodile hunting expedition to New Guinea, Gunther Bahnemann spent a day watching a group of local tribesmen hunting crocodiles. He took his rifle along, probably finding it difficult to believe that he would not be called upon to assist when he heard that the local technique involved nothing more than brute strength.

He watched from one canoe while three tribesmen paddled their canoe towards a crocodile that was sleeping on a mud bank close under the far side of the river. As the tribesmen's canoe neared the crocodile one of the three dropped his paddle and moved quickly into the bow, picking up a short-handled spear as he went. The hunter was completely naked and as the canoe glided along he remained crouched, absolutely still and incredibly tensed. Then, on some hidden signal, the other two hunters suddenly paddled like fury until the canoe rushed past the side of the sleeping crocodile. As it did so the crouching hunter straightened in a split second and leaped out of the canoe and on to the crocodile's back just behind its head. As soon as he had landed he wrapped his legs round the crocodile's body, reached forward and grabbed the tip of the crocodile's upper jaw pulling it up and sideways as hard and as far as he could until it was lodged beneath his armpit. Then, using his other hand, he drew the lower jaw down and out as far as he could until something gave with a tremendous crack – the crocodile's jaws had been dislocated. Then the hunter eased his grip and the crocodile roared and began to beat the mud with its legs and massive tail. By now the canoe had returned and was close to the crocodile's head. One of the men still in the canoe lifted a long, vicious-looking spear and hurled it with all his strength into the crocodile's throat. At that precise moment the man on the crocodile's back flung himself into the canoe and they left the dying crocodile to its own devices. Back in their canoe the three hunters whooped with delight.

Bahnemann had seen many extraordinary things among the tribesmen of New Guinea – who were still officially cannibals – but he had seen nothing to equal this. From the perspective of the twenty-first century the incident also perhaps helps give the lie to the idea that tribal people tend to live in some kind of mutually supportive, idyllic harmony with nature.

Having speared the crocodile the men simply paddled away and when Bahnemann asked his interpreter why the men didn't finish the crocodile off he replied that the tribesmen hated crocodiles so much that, wherever possible, they allowed them to die painfully and slowly.

VERY HIGH DUCK

ESSEX, 1955

Two duck shooters were wandering in an area they'd never shot before. It was the 1950s and there was plenty of duck and goose shooting within thirty miles of the centre of London. These two shooters were down on a holiday from Scotland with their wives and, having pored over a map before they left home, were astonished to discover that they were not doomed to a week sitting idly in a cottage garden or going on day trips from Essex, where the cottage was, to London where their wives were hoping to do a great deal of shopping. No. If they made a few phone calls to the local wildfowling club on that part of the Thames estuary they could probably get a few evenings and early-mornings shooting in. Perfect.

When they arrived at their holiday cottage they found it was pretty enough – so pretty in fact that it put their wives in a good mood and the two men felt they could risk confessing that they'd sneaked their guns and other equipment into the car and were planning to set off for the mud and ooze of the Thames estuary some 25 miles away that very night.

The two wives couldn't have been nicer about it and even offered to make up a few sandwiches and a flask of tea for the two men. At seven o'clock they set off and made it to the prearranged meeting with the local shooting club official who told them where to go on the wide marshes to have the best chance of a duck or two or even a goose. The two men set off and were soon in position. Two hours later they were returning with a duck apiece and highly satisfied with themselves. In fact they were so pleased with the whole thing that they decided to surprise their wives by cooking the two ducks the next day while they were away on a shopping trip. The wives would return exhausted and find a wonderful meal ready and waiting for them.

Next day the two wives set off on their long-awaited shopping trip while the men stayed at home, saying they would potter about the garden or go for a walk. As soon as the women were out of sight they began poring over cookery books to find something suitably elaborate. Two hours later they were in the thick of duck *à l'orange*.

As the duck cooked slowly in the oven the two men noticed a strange smell, rather as if something bad had happened to the drains. They opened a window, made a few jokes about poor quality Essex plumbing and then forgot all about it.

At seven o'clock their wives returned and on entering the kitchen they were met by their husbands' beaming smiles. What the husbands couldn't understand was the look on their wives' faces.

'What on earth is that dreadful smell?' said one.

'Oh it's been like that all day – it's probably the drains,' said her husband.

'But it's appalling.'

'Oh well, don't worry about it,' came the reply. 'We've cooked for you.'

Both wives tried to put a brave face on it and settled down at the beautifully laid table, but however they tried to ignore it the smell got worse, although having lived with it all day the two men now barely noticed it.

When the two duck were brought to the table looking – it has to be said – absolutely perfect, there were smiles all round, but as the carving knife dipped into the first bird the overpowering smell became too much.

'That duck is off,' said one of the wives.

'But it can't be,' said her husband, 'we only shot it last night.'

It was at that moment that the phone rang.

It was the man from the local shooting club who'd allowed the two visitors to shoot.

'How did you get on?' he asked.

'Oh fine – we got a bird apiece. In fact we're just about to eat them.'

'Eat them?' came the reply.

'Yes, that's right.'

'But didn't you see the mark on the map I showed you?'

'What mark was that?'

'The sign that said sewage outfall. All the duck and geese feed there. It's our best spot, but you can't eat anything you shoot there. It's pure sewage.'

And that was the end of the two wives' duck surprise.

DRUNKEN BIRDS

SOMERSET, 1965

In 1965 there was a short-lived series of incidents in which poachers who would normally have used nets or light loads in light shotguns turned to the skilled art of making pheasants drunk.

One West Country poacher took a local journalist along to see how it was done. Before they left the poacher's cottage the journalist saw how barley was soaked in water for a few days. Then the water was drained off and replaced with whisky. After a couple of hours the whisky had all been absorbed and the poacher and journalist set off for the woods. The poacher explained that it was important to take a shotgun so that any passer-by or rambler would simply assume that this was a man out for a walk along the hedgerows in search of a rabbit or two. Most people assume that a man with a shotgun and dressed in the right kind of gear is out shooting perfectly legally. 'It has a lot to do with the fact that they just assume you're a toff – once you've got them thinking that, you know they wouldn't dream of questioning you.'

When the two men reached the edge of a wood the poacher crouched down quickly and took about a pound of the whisky-laden barley grains from a big hidden inner pocket. These were left in a little pile and the poacher then laid a thin trail of single grains from the pile into the wood. As soon as this had been done the two men walked away from the barley trail on the edge of the wood and hid in a ditch from which they kept watch.

The journalist couldn't believe what happened next. At first a few pheasants appeared following the trail of barley grains. Twenty minutes later more than a dozen pheasants were milling around the rapidly diminishing pile of grain, but the journalist noticed that one or two seemed decidedly unsteady on their feet.

Twenty minutes after that, several of the pheasants were squabbling and fighting each other. Others staggered around barely able to stand. One or two were flat on their backs apparently fast asleep. The poacher nodded at the journalist and it was a simple matter for them to cross the field and simply pick each pheasant up and put it in a sack.

WHAT ABOUT THE BEATERS?

RUSSIA, 1978

In the bad old days when Russian Communism kept half Europe under a tyrannical yoke, successive elderly Russian Presidents – Brezhnev in particular – enjoyed the pursuits and pastimes favoured by the tzars they had ousted in 1917. So much so that the ancient woodland areas preserved for Romanov shooting parties were kept just as they'd always been for the new leaders.

Leonid Brezhnev was such an enthusiastic shooter that even in the last years of his life, when he was confined to a wheelchair and barely able to sit up straight, he insisted on being wheeled out to within a few hundred yards of a tethered bear or wolf which, with some assistance from his aides, he would then shoot.

But sporting shooting, like much else in Communist states, was bizarrely organised to say the least. When important guests from the West or from other Communist states were visiting the Russians, they always felt that it was vital to show that Russian Communism could produce a bigger, better shoot than any decadent Western country, but having so little informal contact with the West they failed to understand that the rest of the world had moved on and discovered that size, as they say, isn't everything.

Somehow, too, members of the Politburo had ended up with lives that were as removed from the everyday lives of the people as those of their Romanov predecessors and this was sometimes reflected in their attitude to 'the peasants'.

A visiting Western journalist in 1978, when Russia had become increasingly desperate for foreign currency, was taken to a shoot that the Communist party thought might attract wealthy foreigners. He was told he could either watch or take part and, being a keen shooting man, he thought he might as well have a go.

The senior party members took the whole thing very seriously. There were none of the jokes and banter that normally enliven a formal shoot in England. This was a highly competitive business and the journalist began to think that perhaps the man with the lowest score at the end of the day would be sent to the Gulag for compromising the honour of the Glorious Motherland.

The air was continually black with half grown birds and the guns were continually being bashed on the ankles by hundreds of other birds that were too young to fly but merely dashed past as fast as their legs would carry them. On and on the birds flew overhead, all far too low for a shot. The visiting gun merely watched them go over. Not one was higher than thirty or forty feet.

'My friend,' came the voice of the next gun in the line. 'What is it? You have never seen such sport eh? Are you too astonished to take a few birds. Go on, just fire into the air – you will hit something!'

The journalist was too polite to say that not one of the thousands of birds he had seen was worth shooting. Eventually he plucked up courage.

'Are these birds not a little low?' he shouted.

'But if they are higher we cannot hit so many,' came the amused reply. It was obvious that his neighbour had simply concluded that the journalist was a dimwit, the product of decadent western imperialism.

Lunch was an outrage. A sturgeon at least five feet long lay on a huge table, its caviar spilled on to a huge plate; dozens of bottles of Russian champagne were lined up, together with exotic delicacies from across the world. The journalist saw eating and drinking on a scale he had never even imagined.

The guns drank, ate and drank till they could barely stand.

In the afternoon the journalist spent the whole time watching the guns on either side of him. They were so drunk that they fired wildly at everything. Several times shot whistled dangerously close over the journalist's head. Eventually he lay on the grass flat out and pretended he needed a rest, but in reality he was fearful for his life. If he stayed down, he thought there was a reasonable chance he might end the day without serious gunshot wounds.

The final two drives were the most remarkable of the whole day. A few better birds soared above the journalist's head and he even managed a few shots. Two or three of the other guns had vanished into the woods and at intervals they returned with one of several very attractive girls who'd mysteriously appeared at lunch.

The last drive of the day was the best. Most of the other guns were back in line and seemed to have sobered up. It was a tricky drive as the guns were only eighty yards from the edge of a dense wood that was being driven straight towards them. As soon as he saw the first beater emerge from the wood the journalist stopped shooting.

The gun next to him along the line immediately shouted.

'Why have you stopped shooting? There may yet be birds to come.'

'The beaters are too close,' said the journalist.

'But they are not armed,' came the reply.

The journalist looked towards his fellow shooter, smiling broadly, but the Russian maintained a most serious look. Clearly this was no joking matter.

NATTY DRESSER

HAMPSHIRE, 1984

Shooting tends to produce eccentrics. Mad old colonels – inevitably deaf and usually lame – can be found on obscure and famous shoots from one end of the country to the other, but few could match the extraordinary gentleman who bought a day's shooting at a well-known Hampshire estate in 1984.

Hampshire was and is a very conservative county. At Hampshire shoots the men and women wear Barbours or tweed suits, brogues and gumboots. Some of the guns on this particular day already knew each other when they gathered in the big house for breakfast. Each wore the uniform of the game shooter and none therefore stood out from the herd. True, there were minor variations – one gun had a loden coat which caused a few comments but was just about acceptable. Another, in a fit of sartorial extravagance, wore red gaiters, but that was about the level of rebellion from good dress sense.

Then came the late arrival. He wore orange fireman's trousers about three sizes too big. They only managed to stay up because he also wore fluorescent yellow braces. The gap between the waistband and the man himself was at least a foot and as he walked towards his fellow guests the trousers swayed and circled about him.

On his feet he wore zebra-striped boots with sharp pointed toes. He wore an extremely battered U.S. army jacket with numerous rips and holes through which the stuffing leaked in occasional puffs into the air as he walked.

On his head he wore a fore-and-aft – a gillie's hat – and this was the only thing about him that looked even remotely in keeping with the fabulously expensive Purdey he carried under his arm. But to the seasoned eye even the hat was wrong – it had been the fashion eighty years before and was now rarely seen.

'This is the best shirt ever made for shooting,' he announced, pointing to his chest and introducing himself to his fellow guns.

'Look – just feel, it soaks up any amount of sweat and I've had it for fifty years – hardly a hole in it even now.'

He then pulled out an ancient and very large hip flask and took an enormous swig.

The guns in tweeds and thornproofs were more astonished by the fellow's clipped accent and extremely aristocratic manner than by his bizarre clothing. Who on earth could he be?

Their astonishment increased at the first drive where he continually walked or even darted about within a radius of about ten feet of his peg. He hardly seemed to be concentrating at all, barely looking skywards to see if any birds were coming his way. But when a bird did fly over him his gun was up in a second and down came the bird. By lunchtime he'd hardly missed a thing, taking numerous rights and lefts. On one occasion he managed to reload quickly enough to shoot a bird while another (hit by him seconds earlier) was crashing into the trees behind him.

It was a bravura performance and at lunch the other guns either warmed to him despite his clothing or ignored him completely on the grounds that anyone who dressed so strangely had no right to be such a brilliant shot. At lunch the strange shooter regaled them with tales that suggested he'd shot at some of the best places in the country. Perhaps he was making it all up. No one knew, but somehow it sounded authentic.

The afternoon wore on and after several indifferent drives they came to a drive that usually produced the best birds of the day. The man with the orange trousers declared he was tired and was happy to watch. He gave a young beater his gun and insisted they swap places. The beater, though delighted, was nervous, so the man with the orange trousers helped coach him as the birds came over. He also ran about picking the birds up as if he were a retriever.

At the end of the day, instead of returning to the house with the other guests he said he thought he'd left a wounded bird in some thick undergrowth nearby and set off to retrieve it. The other guns waited for an hour or more at the house – far longer than they would normally wait – but the strange gun never reappeared and he was never seen again at that shoot or, so far as anyone is aware, at any other.

ENTERPRISING DOWN-AND-OUT

LONDON, 1988

In the 1980s there was a short-lived fad among London's tramps for living on the River Thames. Some found themselves little alcoves under the Victorian bridges, others clambered aboard apparently abandoned barges and spent a relatively comfortable few weeks before either the barge owners or the river police discovered what was going on and summarily ejected them.

One enterprising down-and-out gradually built himself a kind of tiny floating village some one hundred yards out into the river in front of the old Greater London Council building just downstream from Westminster Bridge. The 'village' consisted of several platforms made from wooden pallets roped together and kept afloat by empty oil drums. The superstructure appeared to be a series of rooms covered with tarpaulin; other platforms, either directly attached to the main one or connected by narrow walkways, had dozens of pot plants and small trees in tubs; some platforms were piled high with bicycles, old batteries and other junk. One further platform had a dog kennel on it. What went on inside the tarpaulin-covered parts of the structure no one ever knew, but occasionally that first summer the man who'd built the whole thing would strip off and go for a dip in the river. Very craftily he built a tiny platform which he floated off well away from the main structure on a rope. On this he built what he hoped would be an attractive nesting box for ducks. It worked. The wild ducks of the river built their nest in the box and the wild man pinched and ate their eggs.

Further upriver at Kingston another tramp who was clearly impressed by the Westminster man, built a similar platform of bicycles, boxes, old tin baths, oil drums and wooden pallets. His platform – or series of platforms – extended along the river opposite the old power station and a few hundred yards below Kingston bridge. It really did have the appearance of a little village, and like the man at Westminster, the Kingston riverboat man had a vast collection of bicycles and a specially built platform where he obviously hoped ducks would nest. Sadly this was not to be and in an extraordinary turn of events he decided that rather than duck eggs he'd have the ducks themselves.

He was seen on several occasions one sunny autumn day – he at least waited until the season had begun – shooting at ducks winging their way along the river. No one knows how many ducks he bagged, but it was several weeks before the Thames police intervened and discovered that he was using an ancient hammer gun he'd inherited from his grandfather. It was one of the few possessions he'd retained from earlier, more conventional days. In fact it turned out he'd been to Winchester School and started a promising career in the city before something triggered the desire to wander and leave a good job and a promising career.

FELLED BY RABBIT

BEDFORDSHIRE, 1995

Out shooting in Bedfordshire one winter morning in 1995, Tom Westall had already been very unlucky. With a friend he was shooting rabbits over ferrets, or, more precisely, he was trying to shoot rabbits over ferrets. The technique was simple enough. You found a likely looking hole, popped your favourite ferret down it and if any rabbits were in residence they would quickly bolt and that's when you bowled them over with your trusty 12-bore. They'd improved the odds in their favour by blocking all the holes they could find on one side of the bury and most of those on the other side. Tom stood guard over the remaining unblocked holes where, logically, the rabbits would bolt. But this was the third bury they'd tried that morning and not even a whisper of a rabbit.

The ferret went in and they waited as quiet and still as possible. Five minutes passed, ten. Nothing. Then the ferret reappeared and Tom's mate picked it up and put it down a different hole. A minute later it reappeared and was very reluctant to go down a third time – a sure sign that there were no rabbits down there.

Tom and his friend wandered disconsolate across the wide field to a distant hedgerow, complaining about the lack of rabbits and indeed the lack of hedgerows. Certainly since their early days ferreting in Hertfordshire and right across Bedfordshire and Buckinghamshire things had declined dramatically. At first there were too many rabbits, but it was a rabbit-filled world in those days with small fields and thick-grown hedges. Farms were less tidy, less suburban-looking than they were now. Tom admitted that some farmers who'd wiped their rabbits out had asked him to bring a few live ones from distant farms almost as if they were worth restocking. Tom thought this was only sensible. No one wanted every last rabbit to vanish; it would put the old ferreters out of business. For a farmer or a ferreter to try to get rid of every rabbit was a bit like a fox hunter trying to hunt all his foxes to extinction. It was just putting yourself out of business.

'Mind you,' said Tom, 'I've noticed those rabbits definitely getting bigger and more aggressive. I remember when they used to die of fright sometimes when they got caught in a net. But now more of them back up in a tunnel and use their back legs to kick the hell out of the poor old ferret.'

At the next hedgerow they spent twenty minutes blocking the holes, put the ferret down and waited to see what would happen. Suddenly a couple of rabbits bolted. Tom got one and the other got away. Then Tom heard a curious scuffling just inside the entrance to one of the holes. He tiptoed over and knelt down. Still he could hear the scuffling, but neither rabbit nor ferret appeared. A few more minutes passed and still the noise continued. Tom decided to look. He crouched as low as he could and peered into the mouth of the dark hole.

Then suddenly it was as if someone had turned all the lights off and the next thing Tom knew, he was being gently shaken by his friend. He learned later that at the very moment he'd peered into the hole a big buck rabbit had bolted at terrific speed and hit him full in the face. The crash knocked Tom out, but the rabbit – clearly endowed with the thicker skull – rolled over a few times, got back on its feet and disappeared into the distance. Tom's friend had been unable to help him for a full five minutes because he'd been laughing so much.

'As long as I live I'll never see a more amazing sight,' he said later.